Secrets of...

THE FREEPRENEUR

How to build a successful business life… on your terms!

PART ONE: THE MINDSET

Bodo Codreanu

WELFORD PUBLISHING

Published in 2020 by Welford Publishing

Copyright © 2020 Bogdan-Dumitru Codreanu

Paperback ISBN: 978-1-9162671-5-2

Bogdan-Dumitru Codreanu has asserted his right to be identified as the author of this Work in accordance with the Copyright, Designs and Patents Act 1988.

All rights reserved.

No part of this publication may be reproduced, stored in a retrieval system, or transmitted in any form or by any means, electronic, mechanical, photocopying, recording or otherwise, without the prior permission of the copyright owner.

Ghostwriter Cassandra Farren

The Freepreneur™, Freepreneur Business Mindset™, Freepreneur Mindset™, Freepreneur Business Method™, Freepreneur Business Tools™, Freepreneur Startup Method™, Startupers.Club ™ Freepreneur Why Analysis™, The Freepreneur Manifesto™, Freepreneur Academy™ and Freepreneur Courses™ are trademarks of Bogdan Dumitru Codreanu

A catalogue for this book is available from the British Library.

Disclaimer

This book is designed to provide helpful information on the subjects discussed. The information provided in this book is for informational purposes only and is not intended to be a source of advice or credit analysis with respect to the material presented. The information and/or documents contained in this book do not constitute legal or financial advice and should never be used without first consulting with a financial professional to determine what may be best for your individual needs.

The publisher and the author do not make any guarantee or other promise as to any results that may be obtained from using the content of this book. You should never make any investment decision without first consulting with your own financial advisor and conducting your own research and due diligence. To the maximum extent permitted by law, the publisher and the author disclaim any and all liability in the event any information, commentary, analysis, opinions, advice and/or recommendations contained in this book prove to be inaccurate, incomplete or unreliable, or result in any investment or other losses.

Content contained or made available through this book is not intended to and does not constitute legal advice or investment advice and no attorney-client relationship is formed. The publisher and the author are providing this book and its contents on an "as is" basis. Your use of the information in this book is at your own risk. Although the publisher and the author have made every effort to ensure that the information in this book was correct at press time and while this publication is designed to provide accurate information in regard to the subject matter covered, the publisher and the author assume no responsibility for errors, inaccuracies, omissions, or any other inconsistencies herein and hereby disclaim any liability to any party for any loss, damage, or disruption caused by errors or omissions, whether such errors or omissions result from negligence, accident, or any other cause.

This publication is meant as a source of valuable information for the reader, however it is not meant as a substitute for direct expert assistance. If such level of assistance is required, the services of a competent professional should be sought.

This book is not intended as a substitute for the medical advice of physicians. The reader should regularly consult a physician in matters relating to his/her health and particularly with respect to any symptoms that may require diagnosis or medical attention.

Some names and identifying details could have been changed to protect the privacy of the individuals and I may have changed some identifying characteristics such as physical properties, occupations and places of residence.

Dedication

For my dad, the brightest star in the sky…

Preface

When I flew into London to attend a Professional Speakers Association meeting on the 8th of February 2020, I already had a deep knowing. A knowing that, finally, this would be the year when my first book would be written and published. What I didn't know was that a *random* conversation later that day would not only change the direction of my book, but also how I run my business. And as a result of changing how I run my business, I have now changed the way in which I live my life…

You will find out more about these profound changes later in this book, but for now I want to share a bit more about the *random* conversation which took place with an amazing ghost-writer and book mentor, named Cassandra. It's strange how the 'Universe' works. When we began chatting, I told her that I wanted to write a business book that every start-up or serial entrepreneur, I believe, needs. But it turned out that ghostwriting business books weren't her specialty. She explained that she was a heart-led ghostwriter and that her strength was to write powerful books, directly from the heart.

After a more in-depth conversation, my knowing had gone to another level. I knew that the book within me, and the message I wanted to share, was so much more than I ever could have imagined.

I flew back to Bucharest, and a few weeks later my heart-led book began to evolve. At first it evolved into a quarter of the book representing the mindset traits that a Freepreneur needs to win in business life. But there was so much content to share that this quickly turned into half of the book, before I finally made the decision for the entire book to focus on how to create The Mindset of The Freepreneur.

Six months and many (healing) tears later, there are now over 30,000 words which share the 20 most powerful mindset traits of a successful business owner. I call them 'Secrets'.

I believe the Business Method is also an essential part of every entrepreneur's journey to become a Freepreneur, but I will share it in the second book of this trilogy.

For now, I'm looking forward to sharing my mindset secrets with you. I hope you enjoy them, and that you too will embrace the *random* - and sometimes unexpected - twists and turns in your life.

Enough is enough!

Let's be honest. You're feeling frustrated that your future business plans haven't come to fruition. You've long held this dream of becoming a successful entrepreneur, yet no matter how hard you try, it still feels out of reach.

Maybe you have already started your business, you are working hard, but you are also working every hour that God sends, and you're tired. You knew it wasn't going to be easy, but you're already questioning why it has to be so difficult. Maybe you haven't got what it takes? Do you really have enough time to finish what you've started? Is it possible to find more hours in the day when you're already feeling so exhausted? How will you manage to get everything set up and in place when there's so much to learn? Perhaps you should stick with what you know and rely on the 'security' of an employed position? The majority of your friends and family don't seem to support your decision to go it alone, so perhaps it would be for the best. Maybe if you just watch one more webinar or sign up for one more life-changing seminar, *then* you'll have the missing piece and your business will finally fall into place?

I understand the feeling of constant overwhelm. You feel like you are taking one step forward and three steps back. You're tired of not making progress, and instead of taking inspired action, you're now overthinking everything and have become a master of procrastination.

Give yourself a break and know that these feelings, thoughts, and doubts are completely normal, but it doesn't have to be this way. I want you to trust that wherever you are on your journey is exactly where you need to be.

Perhaps you are working as an employee and you are feeling frustrated with the restricted limits of what you can achieve or frustrated on not being paid as expected. Maybe you have already started working hard on your entrepreneurial journey, but it hasn't gone to plan. You're feeling overwhelmed and disappointed with your results. Or you have been running a successful business before losing everything, and you now feel like it's the end of the world as you know it. You're wondering when there will be more abundance, joy, and happiness in your life.

I have written this book to support and guide you, whilst helping you to find the freedom and the answers you've been seeking. I've worked with thousands of entrepreneurs and I've never met anyone who has all the answers. That's not how it works.

I want you to feel proud of yourself for wanting to create a successful business life, on your terms. In doing this, you not only have the opportunity to change your own life, but to also make a difference to many other people's lives – not to mention the huge reward of achieving freedom and personal fulfilment.

Will the highs and lows ever end?

The journey of an entrepreneur is like being on a rollercoaster; your ride begins from the moment you decide you want more from your life. You may want more money, more quality time, more holidays, more friends, more life experiences, more joy, more fun, more fulfilment… but ultimately you want more freedom to live life on your terms. I know that you have these desires, and I congratulate you for wanting to make them happen. I also know that, right now, the ride feels more exhausting than exhilarating!

This journey is not for the fainthearted. It takes smart work, focus, and determination, to become a Freepreneur and, contrary to some beliefs, it does not happen overnight! You have to learn, evolve, and adapt at every stage of your journey. Those who don't learn, evolve, and adapt, will become stuck. Simple. So, I have some good news and some bad news.

The bad news is that overwhelm, caused by fear, is the biggest reason why entrepreneurs do not become Freepreneurs.

The good news is that I will be sharing all of my powerful Secrets of The Freepreneur with you, so that by the end of this book you can say goodbye to overwhelm and say hello to business success, as well as a sense of fulfilment and freedom!

Sounds great, right? But hang on a minute. Before we begin, you may well be asking, 'Who is Bodo Codreanu? What does he know about building a successful business life on his terms? And more importantly, does he *really* understand what it feels like to decide enough is enough?'

Let me take you back to summer 2011…

How could you be so stupid!? You're an idiot, a complete failure. As I lay alone on the sofa, my anger continued to build and the vile voice in my head continued to torment me. I had never felt so ashamed in my whole life. Not only had I let myself down, but I had let my family down. I was meant to be the man of the family, the one who protected them, the one who provided for them. And I wanted to be a success, but in reality, all I'd succeeded in doing was being a complete disappointment. It hurt me to think that even the people close to me were questioning my decisions, but who could blame them?

Everything had happened so quickly, and we were all in shock that it had come to this. Part of me wanted to run away, but that wasn't going to happen. How could I run when even standing up from the sofa took all of my strength? Would I ever recover from this? Would the guilt and the shame ever subside? All I had ever wanted was to become a successful entrepreneur and to build an empire. Instead, I was now deeply buried under the rubble of my own ruins. How on earth did my life come to this?

Just a few months earlier, in December 2010, at the age of 30, I appeared to have it all. With three apartments, two cars, a great reputation, and a thriving business, I thought I was living the dream. I enjoyed an affluent life with my wife and young family. You know what they say about business owners: work hard and play hard. And I did both. I would often work from morning until midnight, always striving towards my next goal. I was telling myself that I was living my best life, but despite the many exotic holidays and the luxurious lifestyle, the cracks were beginning to show.

I had set out on my entrepreneurial journey aged 25. I had been steadily climbing the corporate ladder, but I became disillusioned, feeling like I was playing a real-life game of snakes and ladders. I'd worked hard, but instead of being rewarded for my efforts, my boss had decided this wasn't enough. Instead of keeping my salary in line with my results, he thought it was fair to pay me less than I was already earning. How was that fair? I felt angry and trapped as I realised that I had built something that wasn't mine. I tried to negotiate, but the final decision was out of my hands. So, I decided that enough was enough and that if I was going to work hard, from now on it would be ON MY TERMS.

Over the next six years I set up two businesses – one selling electrical equipment on my own; the other one with a group of founders. I started my first business with a small loan of less than $2000 and an action plan written on a piece of scrap paper! Yet I grew this from zero to the first million dollars in revenue in less than five years.

I will share later in this book how I started and grew the company, but for now I will say that my profits were increasing, my employee numbers were growing, and success was well within reach. That was when I expanded and built the second company – in the same field, but with three partners. In less than one year, we achieved over a million dollars in revenue. We had suppliers from all over the world, we had built our product brand, and had thousands of happy customers throughout the country.

Everything may have looked great, but I could feel that something was missing, I didn't admit this to anyone else, let alone to myself, but despite looking like I had my life together I didn't truly feel fulfilled. Little did I know that this would be the least of my problems…

As my businesses grew, so did the size of my contracts. Part of my dream was to expand, but in reality, an increase in scale also meant an increase in risk. This threat started to become apparent after the financial crisis hit Romania in 2009, when my largest clients started to pay me late. In the beginning, there was minimal business disruption, but it wasn't long before my company was losing money due to poor money collection from my clients.

I knew I couldn't ignore the problem or bury my head in the sand, so I swallowed my pride and travelled across the country to meet up with every supplier that my company owed money to. I explained the situation and, with my reputation preceding me, they all agreed that I could rearrange payment terms so that my business could continue to trade. After everything was in place, I felt exhausted, but I breathed a sigh of relief that everyone had been so accommodating and I felt positive that everything would be ok. My final meeting was when I spoke to the landlord of my business premises to re-negotiate the terms of the rent payment. Thankfully, he also agreed, and for the first time in months I slept without worrying. This was just a short-term challenge – or so I thought.

The next day, I woke up feeling refreshed and was looking forward to working on my business instead of in my business. I arrived at my premises with a spring in my step but felt confused to find that the front door was locked! Why was it locked? I felt a bit panicked but told myself that everything would be ok. Surely it had to be a mistake!? A phone call to my business landlord told me that there was no mistake. He would not be allowing me to enter my showroom until he had received his rent in full.

My heart sank as my anger surged. No way was I going to allow this to happen! Yes, I was having a temporary cash flow problem, but why had he taken such extreme action? Especially as we had agreed the contract terms. I was entitled to go in, so I decided to enter the premises whether he liked it or not. With all my might, I forced the door open – and before I knew it, the police arrived! Thankfully, I showed them the contract and they agreed that I had the right to enter.

By this time, some security guards from the building had turned up, along with a crowd of people wondering what the hell was going on! Part of me felt ashamed, but I wasn't going to admit defeat. How was I meant to keep my promises to my suppliers and customers and employees if I couldn't gain access to my own office or stock? It was like a scene out of a movie. Part of me was crying on the inside, trying not to allow my fear to take over, but the other part of me wasn't going to give up without a fight.

After realising there was no way to gain access, I had to walk away from the building that day. But two sleepless nights later, I went back again, determined to finish what I'd started. I forced the door again, driven by the rage within me; I was so scared of losing everything I'd worked so hard for. The security alarms sounded and, minutes later, more security guards arrived in cars that had been sent to prevent me from entering. I called the police again but was told they couldn't do anything to help me.

As my physical strength subsided, I knew I couldn't fight them. What was I meant to do? I walked away and went back into my apartment feeling so afraid. Over the next two months, I tried my hardest to pay the bills by trying to find new suppliers, but when they found out that the cheques I was writing were not being honoured, nobody wanted to trade with me. They had all lost their trust in me. My company now had a bad reputation along with bad credit records – not a great combination.

I knew I had to keep trying, so I contacted my other company which was being run by my partners. But surprise! As soon as they heard the news that I had experienced some trouble, they wanted to completely remove me from the company. From boom to bust in the blink of an eye! I had never felt so alone. As if by magic, none of my friends would take my calls. It seemed that they didn't want to be associated with such a failure. The few who did answer were not interested in how they might be able to support me; they were more interested in how I could help them. Nice!

The pressure was building, and I felt like I was suffocating while everything in my life was falling apart. It wasn't just my business and my relationship that were slipping away; I felt like I was losing my mind.

The bank found out I was in financial difficulty and sent a representative to my home because my company loans were secured against my personal assets. I was instructed to sign a document which meant I had no choice but to give all of my assets to the bank in just 30 days' time! My apartments, my mum's apartment, my cars… everything. Where were we going to live? How would we survive? My head wouldn't stop spinning as I collapsed onto the sofa where I barely moved for the next three weeks.

In the beginning, the downwards spiral seemed to have no end, but there were two glimmers of hope which were the first steps to help get me back on my feet. The first was a book I received on the same day as my landlord blocked the entry to my building. When I had ordered it, I hadn't known the full extent of the damage that was to follow. I just knew that I had made some mistakes in my business, and I wanted to learn from them and never to make them again. So, when the book *Entrepreneurship* by Marius Ghenea arrived, there was a part of me that knew this was going to form part of my new foundations.

The first words I read were from a review on the back cover from Doug Richard that said, '*I always said that entrepreneurship could be taught and should be learned.*' This was one of those face-palm moments when I felt like an idiot! Everything I had done in my business had been led by the feeling in my gut, not from the strategy in my head.

This book sparked the idea that an accelerated learning process could be put in place to create a strong and sustainable business by using a system which could prevent other business owners from making the same mistakes that I had. I don't think it was a coincidence that I received this book when I did, or that it was the first serious book on entrepreneurship that was written by a Romanian entrepreneur. The book is described as *'The road from ideas to opportunities when running a successful business'*. At that point I had no idea where my own road was leading, but it gave me a renewed sense of optimism.

The second glimmer of hope was when a family member offered us an apartment to rent for an affordable monthly payment. Compared with the brand-new penthouse we had been in the process of furnishing, it was far from the same standard, but in that moment, I was so grateful to be given an opportunity to start again. I had read about other entrepreneurs who had lost millions (and others even billions) before rebuilding their empire. If they could do it, so could I! After three weeks of feeling sorry for myself, I was sick of the negative emotions I'd been tormenting myself with. Enough was enough! I wasn't sure how I was going to get back on my feet, but the first step to get myself out of the black hole was to move to another house.

I wouldn't say I felt full of excitement, but going to view the new apartment had given me some much-needed hope. It wasn't too far from where we lived, but there was one slight challenge. The previous tenants had been asked to paint all of the rooms before they moved out, and they had followed the instructions and painted the whole apartment in… pink! I know they say that beggars can't be choosers, but I could not see myself settling into a new life whilst every room was painted pink! There were only ten days remaining until my old apartment was being handed over to the bank. It was going to be tight, but as I had some white paint left from some other projects, I decided to take matters into my own hands, literally.

I set to work and was making good progress until I reached the big wall between the kitchen and the living room. It was not only covered in pink paint, but it was coated from top to bottom in thick, sticky grease underneath all of the paint! I began painting over it but the next day I found big holes where the paint had sunk in from the moisture. The next day I painted over it again, but the following day the same problem occurred. More paint and more bloody holes.

I continued this relentless cycle for three long days until I phoned my cousin and pleaded with him for help. Time was running out and I wanted to get everything finished before the furniture was being moved in. His advice was that I needed to strip the paint right back to the concrete wall before washing it down and repainting it. Upon hearing his advice, my heart sank. Really? Had all of my hard work gone to waste? It took me two further days of persistent scrubbing and I felt so frustrated at times that I cried, but I didn't give up. I finally succeeded by washing the wall down and giving it one last coat of paint.

I'd done it, and it was the best-looking wall in the house!

You may be wondering why I'm sharing what could seem like a small, insignificant moment with you, but for me this was when everything changed. I had worked so hard for ten days solid. I had overcome challenges. I had pushed through the pain and I had finally accomplished my goal! I remember thinking to myself, *with these two hands I can do good things*. My mental state had changed, and I was ready to embrace the next chapter of my life.

Having tried to put the pieces back together, it turned out that our marriage couldn't be rebuilt. But what could be rebuilt were the foundations for the rest of my life. Later that year, I started some new businesses as a marketing affiliate; I set up an online store and an electrical equipment store. In this process, I discovered that I could set up companies in different industries with minimal investment.

Whilst all of this was happening, I was on a mission behind the scenes to learn everything that I could about successful entrepreneurs. I read many books and attended as many seminars as I could on my quest for knowledge. In 2012, 18 months on from the collapse of my first business, I found myself at a seminar run by a man who was teaching 300 people how to become an entrepreneur. Sounds good, right? That was until I realised that his first business was teaching others how to start and run a business! I remember looking around the hall and thinking that all of these entrepreneurs could get something better than this for the same investment. I wanted to be the person who guided them; I wanted to be on that stage. This was my purpose!

As I started to connect the dots backwards, I could see that everything I had been through in my life had been good preparation. But I didn't just want good. I wanted great. I wanted to be the most successful entrepreneurship influencer in Europe.

Right now, you might be thinking: a) Was that your ego talking? and b) That's a huge goal! But I can assure you that my vision came straight from my soul. When I declared that I wanted to be 'the most successful', this meant that I would have helped the most business owners to achieve their own version of success. And yes, you're right, it was and still is a huge goal for me in the present moment as I write this book.

I wasn't under any illusion that this would be achieved overnight. In fact, I made a long list of everything that I felt I needed to add to my base of business skills and knowledge, and set the date of achieving this by 2025. I felt fired up after the seminar and got to work on my list.

One of my tasks was to complete an MBA. Not only did I accomplish this in 2015, but I also competed against over 1000 people to be awarded a fully funded Executive MBA scholarship! Other tasks included completing a train the trainer course, along with a train the trainer master course, and a personal development counsellor course, to name just a few.

It might surprise you that other tasks on my list included working in one medium and one large company as an employee. Why? I wanted to fully understand the process of building and sustaining a successful business. I will admit that several people in my life were encouraging me to 'play it safe' and, to be honest, there was a part of me that liked the 'freedom' of not having to worry about the company profits and paying myself and others every month. But no matter how hard I tried to fit into this mould, my soul wasn't there.

Have you ever had a time in your life when the perfect sign arrives for you at the perfect time? At the end of 2016, I was still working through my list when I saw an online advert that spoke straight to my heart.

Do you have big dreams? Are you creative and innovative? Do you want to change the world?

Yes, yes, and yes! I clicked the link to the website where I found the details for a 3-month international educational programme on how to create a business from an idea. To apply for a place on the programme, I needed to spend one hour filling out an application. So, I entered all of the information, and was looking forward to finding out if I had succeeded in receiving my interview call. They said that I would find out in the next 48 hours. 48 hours passed, no call. Four days later, still no call. I sent a polite reminder to ask when it would take place, but I'll be honest, my head was screaming, *come on, what are you waiting for? Let's get on with this, some people have life-changing goals to achieve!*

It was 24 hours later when I finally had my interview. After five minutes of answering questions about myself, the interviewer interrupted me and said, 'Stop!' I was shocked. Had I said something wrong? The words that came out of his mouth shocked me even more. 'Bodo, you don't need to be a student. You have achieved so much already that you should also be a mentor and a trainer!' Wow, really? Oh, ok then!

A few weeks later I was on my way to the Sorbonne in Paris, where I was invited to be a part of the seminar as a mentor, with a view to duplicating their business system in Romania. I sat in the workshop room watching in awe at the slides that were being presented. 90% of the information I recognised; this was exactly how I had built my own companies. The remaining 10% of the slides were the real eye-openers. It was this information that I wished I'd had access to when my first company went bust. If I had had access to this information, who knows how many mistakes I could have avoided and how my story may have ended?

As you can imagine, after my trip I was even more motivated to achieve my mission, but I was still working as an employee Monday to Friday, 9am -6pm. My mentor set me tasks to complete, so I was working towards my dream during the evenings and weekends. The plan was to research and plan a seminar that I would run in Romania, but I would be teaching under the name of my mentor's institution. Unfortunately, or you could say fortunately, this didn't go to plan. After several weeks, it became apparent that we wouldn't be working together in this way. It would have been easy to have felt disheartened, but over the next few months I continued to work hard and smart on making my dream a reality.

This was when I remembered that Marian Rujoiu, my mentor from the train the trainer master course had promised to support me by promoting my first seminar to his list of clients. I felt excited knowing that the wheels were in motion, but what if nobody registered?

I needn't have worried. After just a few hours of the email being sent, I received the news that 90 people had already registered! Was there a mistake? 90 people wanted to come to MY Start-up Mastery Weekend Seminar. Yes, it was free, but that wasn't the point. This was really happening. Maybe, just maybe this could work!

Just to be sure I wasn't dreaming, I arranged for every registered participant to receive a phone call to check their attendance, and guess what? 80% of them confirmed! I knew then that I had a big decision to make… and I resigned from my job! Some people may think that was a big risk, but I needed to cut the 'security' and trust that this was my true path. My partner at the time supported my decision, and we knew that despite it being tight, our bills would be covered for at least six months until the money from my business would start to come in as my clients increased.

In May 2017, I followed my heart, ran the seminar, and then ran with the opportunity to create a successful business life on my terms. I was even more determined to develop a movement of Freepreneurs who would make a difference in the world. On their terms.

The reason that I was so keen to quickly work with entrepreneurs was to understand whether what worked for me would work for others. I started to give free and paid seminars with the belief that the single most important thing that a Freepreneur needed was a step-by-step method to create a successful business. This is very important, and as a result I attracted a steady flow of one-to-one coaching clients. But what became apparent was that the method alone wasn't enough. I had to ask myself how I could serve them better. And I decided that the support from a Freepreneur also needed the support from other like-minded people, to help them boost their results by receiving invaluable feedback from each other. This is what inspired me to set up live classes in groups.

The classes attracted different client avatars and helped me to understand that I could serve entrepreneurs at any stage of their journey. This was great progress, but I observed that some people were getting their desired results, whilst others weren't. I took some time to analyse why this was and discovered that there was yet another missing piece: a Freepreneur needs to use the perfect and proper business tools! To build and scale a business, I taught all three elements, and once again achieved great feedback and great results – again for the majority. But for me, the majority wasn't enough. I wanted 100% customer satisfaction, and with this in mind I was determined to find the final missing piece.

A Freepreneur needs a liberated mindset. And it took blood, sweat, tears, and working directly with over 1000 entrepreneurs over three long years, but *finally* I had discovered the secret formula that, when implemented, takes an ordinary entrepreneur to a Freepreneur – someone who lives a successful business life on their terms. So, you can safely say that I definitely understand what it's like to decide that enough is enough.

I have openly shared my journey because I want you to know that highs and lows are not necessarily a negative part of your journey; it's how you manage them that matters. Well, more to the point, it's how you manage yourself that really matters. Right here, right now, I want you to decide that enough is enough.

It's time to trust the process, take a step back, and understand that you cannot fail when you master my method of how to become a Freepreneur.

Freepreneur mindset + support + business method + business tools = The Freepreneur.

I want you to trust that you have my book in your hands for a reason. Hold on tight, enjoy the ride, and know that you haven't come this far only to come this far.

Are you ready to build a successful business life on your terms? Are you ready to become a Freepreneur?

Let's do this!

Where do you begin?

First and foremost, to become a Freepreneur you must master The Freepreneur Mindset.

As soon as you've grasped this concept, your entrepreneurial journey will become so much smoother. When you make positive shifts in your internal world, you will see the positive shifts reflect back in your external world – not only in your business, but also in your personal life. What's not to love?

Your business starts with you.

One of the biggest challenges is shifting your mindset to believe that you can become a successful business owner. I'm telling you this because I know that you have the potential to achieve your goal of running a successful business, or else you wouldn't have come this far.

But first you need to understand that where you are right now isn't serving you. It's said that we have between 60-80k thoughts per day, and I am guessing that many of yours are currently spinning out of control. Even when you do manage to take one step forward, it then feels like you take two or three steps back!

I understand that you may have read that last sentence twice and wondered if we are on the same page, literally. And I can hear that little voice in your head that may have asked, 'Bodo, what do you mean I need to have a Freepreneur mindset?'

So, let me explain…

I get it, and when I set up my first business, I would have asked exactly the same question. In fact, I probably would have laughed and dismissed this 'mindset malarkey' as being a load of wishy-washy rubbish! If you had any blocks come up about mindset, I want you to know that this is ok, but I'm asking you to read on with an open mind. Why? Because if I'm completely honest with you, not having an open mind was one of the biggest mistakes I made in the past. I was more interested in fast cars, fast results, and fast profits.

Whilst building my empire, I failed to notice that my not-so-solid foundations were suddenly sinking in the sand. I wrongly believed that me and my business were two separate entities. Yes, legally they were separate, but this is where I and many other entrepreneurs fell down. If you fail to see that your business starts with your mindset or choose to ignore this part of the process, you will hit many brick walls in your business. They may come in the form of financial, marketing, or scaling up challenges, and if you think you're feeling frustrated now, let me tell you this: your frustration will escalate tenfold if you choose not to strengthen your most important asset – your mindset.

You will remember from my story the real-life wall that almost pushed me over the edge. It took all my strength and courage to strip everything back to basics because the holes were absorbing all of the fresh new paint I'd added. Imagine that your wall is your business and the holes are your negative beliefs. Like it or not, if you don't strip everything back and make a fresh start, you will constantly be leaking negative beliefs, which will never provide a solid foundation for a strong and sustainable business.

So, what exactly is The Freepreneur?

It's my pleasure to share my secrets with you and before we begin, I would like to share my ultimate definition…

The Ultimate Definition

The Freepreneur is an entrepreneur with an investor attitude* as opposed to the attitude of the employee.

*an investor:

- Chooses carefully why, where, when, with whom and how to invest their resources
- Aims for the lowest risk and investment against the highest return possible
- Chooses evergreen instead of ephemeral
- Feeds their wallet and starves their ego
- Chooses freedom instead of control

Secret #1

The Freepreneur loves and accepts themself unconditionally

Perhaps this isn't the first piece of guidance you were expecting? Let me explain. In this day and age, the majority of people walk around wearing a metaphorical mask, proudly sharing the rose-tinted highlights of their life on social media, filtering photographs of themselves whilst pretending to be #livingtheirbestlife.

I am not sharing this to berate social media. In fact, I love social media and the power it holds for our businesses, but I have seen first-hand the impact of not being true to yourself and pretending to be someone that you're not. Instead of increasing your self-love, you are eating away at your self-worth.

Let's be honest, the fear of not feeling good enough has consumed us all at some point. This can stem from your childhood; perhaps it was the mean teacher whose words you still carry around with you, or maybe it was the belittling words from your boss, or from someone you were in a relationship with. It's not relevant who it was or what they said, but what is important is the interpretation of the words and how you allow these words to impact your behaviour and your life right now. The key word in that sentence is *allow*. Whatever was said has been and gone. We can't change the past, but if you are still believing and allowing these words to shape your future business, then who has the power? Spoiler alert: It's not you!

If you are already carrying around wounds from your past, then not loving and accepting yourself can quickly escalate as your journey as an entrepreneur progresses. The constant pressure you put on yourself, your constant need to be the best, along with the constant desire to prove yourself to others, is not a great combination. When I was starting out on my journey, I was completely oblivious to the hidden cracks underneath the surface. Looking back, I can see that if I had truly loved and accepted myself from the beginning then there's a good chance that the mistakes that I made may not have happened.

Loving yourself is not a quick fix solution, it's something that takes time, but I want you to know that it's possible. I would like to add here that loving yourself doesn't mean becoming arrogant or shouting from the rooftops that you are the greatest, or that you are head over heels love with yourself! In fact, I believe that if you truly are in love, or falling in love, with yourself, then these statements are not necessary. You will know the feeling of love; this feeling will reflect in your actions, and this will reflect in your energy to those around you. Sometimes no words are needed.

Reclaim the love that was always yours and you will be rewarded with a business, as well as relationships, which will grow with joy and ease!

Secret #2

The Freepreneur lets go of grudges

The first step is to forgive anyone who, in your opinion, has hurt or upset you, which has led to you inadvertently punishing yourself by not loving yourself unconditionally. Even the thought of forgiveness can bring up a barrier, and you may be wondering why you should have to be the one to forgive.

Let's have a look at the definition of forgiveness.

Psychologists generally define forgiveness as a conscious, deliberate decision to release feelings of resentment or vengeance toward a person or group who has harmed you, regardless of whether they actually deserve your forgiveness. Forgiveness does not mean forgetting, nor does it mean condoning or excusing offences.

The way I see it is that once you release the hate in your heart, this creates the space for the love and acceptance which you crave. Once you begin to embrace this shift in perspective, you will start to release the subconscious blocks that were playing out in your life as self-loathing thoughts and self-destructing habits.

The second step is to forgive yourself. You may be asking why you would need to forgive yourself. The simple answer is that by feeling angry at yourself for the perceived mistakes or choices you've made, you are not loving, accepting, or treating yourself in the way you deserve. It's important to start where you are and not to add conditions such as 'I'll love myself more once I start my business, or I'll accept that I'm a success once I make my first sale'. No matter how quickly your business grows on the outside, the cracks from the inside will appear sooner or later if you don't build your foundations on the grounds of self-acceptance and self-love.

Forgive yourself now and you will easily forgive others!

Secret #3

The Freepreneur is defined by their present

Despite many of the world's greatest entrepreneurs coming from families that were poor, there is still a negative belief that if you didn't have much money growing up, then you are not destined to be successful. There's been an invisible battle going on in your head and you want to break free from your past, but at the same time you subconsciously fear abandonment if you find the financial freedom that you seek. There is an inherent fear of those close to you not understanding your new way of living and the new choices you've made.

I experienced this for the first time when I was just ten years old. Having spent the first ten years of my life growing up in Romanian communism, my family did not have much money. I cherished life's little luxuries, such as the weekly newspaper my grandmother would receive. When the communism ended, many people were on strike, which meant that if you lived in the outskirts of the city there was no way of receiving a newspaper. Or was there?

In 1990, I spent all of my pocket money buying newspapers and delivering them to the smaller communities for a higher price. I felt proud of myself that I had helped others and also made some money, but my parents weren't in agreement. I was told not to be so stupid and that I needed to stop this venture immediately as people might laugh at our family. They told me, 'We are a family of employees and not the kind of people who take advantage of others' needs.'

I felt ashamed and abruptly put an end to my first taste of the business world. And now I can see how this fear of being ridiculed and breaking free from my family's financial story led me to repeat this destructive pattern later in my life. Through a deep fear of abandonment, I self-sabotaged my own financial success. It wasn't an easy lesson to learn, but by becoming aware of it and changing my own subconscious programming, I have now been able to break free from this cycle.

Deep down we all long for acceptance, but until you find the courage to leave your past in the past, a repetitive pattern of self-sabotage can play out. Your business will be affected unless you choose to push through any discomfort and make the decision to shine your light regardless. It's time to stop wondering what other people will think of you, and time to start taking inspired action towards building your future, your way.

I want you to know that your past does not define you. It is normal that your business and personal growth is going to cause some initial discomfort to those around you. This isn't your problem. Everyone has the opportunity to be the best they can be. Everyone has the choice to play it safe or to strive for the best. Your past has no hold over you… unless you allow it to. You are not your story!

Leave your past in the past!

Secret #4

The Freepreneur releases any negativity from their life

I wouldn't be telling the truth if I told you that you will never lose a friendship, or family member, or relationship, whilst you're on your entrepreneurial journey. As you continue to strive to be the best you can be, not only will your present situation change but your energy will also change. There will be some people who aren't so understanding of your new choices, and that's ok.

I shared in my introduction that I lost many friends when my first business collapsed. At the time I felt upset, and I questioned over and over again what I'd done wrong. Yes, I admit that I made some poor business choices, but this didn't mean that I was a bad person. After tormenting myself for far too long, I had to tell myself that not everyone who started this journey with me would end this journey with me.

Have you heard about the 3 SWs? Some Will, Some Won't, So What! This isn't me being flippant; I'm just being realistic, so that if this does happen to you, you will understand that you're not alone. I believe that everyone who enters or leaves your life does so for a reason. When you find the courage to cut the unnecessary ties when needed, and know that this is all part of your journey, it will stop you from wasting energy on being weighed down by others who need to continue on their own path.

I want you to know that by not being defined by your past, and stepping confidently into your future, you will be creating a ripple of empowerment that will inspire many others. The people who genuinely love you will feel proud of you for being true to yourself, and they will have even more respect that you are forging your own path and creating a new way of wealth. It's realistic that there may be some adjustments in the relationship, but if it's meant to be, you will both become stronger because you decided not to settle. Trust that as you learn to let go of anything that no longer serves you, there will be an increase in growth business and a renewed sense of purpose in both your business as well as your personal relationships.

Trust in the power of letting go!

Secret #5

The Freepreneur celebrates the success of others

When you are living in a place of lack, it is easy to feel angry and resentful towards others who are living an abundant life and appear to have it all. How dare they have success! If they are rich, they must be also be greedy and arrogant! Look at them taking money from other people whilst not having a care in the world!

Admit it, you've had some of these thoughts at some point in your life – most likely whilst you were unhappy with your life and were broke. They may have stemmed from your upbringing or the conditioning we all receive from the mass media. I'm not sharing this principle to play the blame game, but more to raise the point that not correcting this outdated false belief will put a stop to your success.

I will admit that despite being one of those who appeared to have it all, as soon as I lost it I became very bitter towards many people. I hated the representatives at the bank who demanded I hand back my assets; I hated the suppliers who were trying to sue me for the money I owed; and most of all I hated the landlord who blocked the entry to my business premises which, as you know, was the final straw in causing my kingdom to collapse. It took a lot of time and emotional maturity for me to understand this very simple principle: business is business. Nothing more, nothing less.

I very much doubt those people sat down and had a meeting where they all said, 'We don't like Mr Codreanu. Let's cause him hell and make his business go bust!'

I was the one who gave this situation meaning. I was the one who took their decisions personally. Maybe they also had debts to pay? Maybe they had even bigger personal problems than I did? I will never know the truth about what was happening behind the scenes, but I do know that it's irrelevant. Business is business, money is money.

Rich people are rich for a reason. The reason is not because they are lucky, but because they have worked hard on themselves and they don't have the mindset blocks and false beliefs that everyone living in lack has acquired. Do you really believe that you can truly become successful if you despise successful people? Why would your subconscious mind allow you to achieve this?

Once you begin to identify and become aware of this belief, you'll be surprised at how quickly you can change it. I am speaking from experience when I say that it feels so much better to celebrate other people's success. Once you achieve success in your business, you will find other people will celebrate yours, too.

Be kind. What goes around comes around!

Secret #6

The Freepreneur trusts in themself as well as others

If you don't trust yourself in everyday life, then it's unlikely that you'll trust yourself in business. If you don't trust yourself in business, then your business won't continue to grow. You will know if you don't trust yourself, because you will be having a lot of self-doubts, constantly wondering if you are good enough or whether you should succumb to the pressure and get an employed job. As a Freepreneur, you constantly have to make decisions; if you procrastinate or stall, this can stop your success. And there is a lot of pressure when you work alone. What if you make the wrong decision? What if you make the wrong choice? You want to move forward, but instead, that little voice in your head cheering you on appears to have become your worst enemy.

You don't need to walk around wearing a T-shirt saying, 'I don't trust myself'. Your customers will sense it and your sales will reflect this. You may find that you are making money, but it's always 'just enough'; or you've accomplished some great achievements, but you always find yourself dwelling on the things that went wrong. Perhaps you have not always been a trustworthy person yourself, or made a promise or a commitment that you didn't keep? Whatever the root cause, and however it is showing up in your life, you don't need to berate yourself any more or it will cause even more stress and anxiety which escalates the problem.

I am speaking from experience, having lost all trust in myself when I found myself staring into space on the sofa in my lowest moment. In that moment, I not only didn't trust myself – I hated myself, felt ashamed of myself, and certainly didn't feel worthy of achieving much in my life. If only I had known back then that not trusting myself was connected to not loving myself, and that the first step to building up my trust and my life was to begin to love myself, regardless of the perceived mistakes I had made. And it's the same for you.

Not trusting yourself is one block. But not trusting others brings a whole new problem. There's no getting away from it, whether it's in your business or in your personal life – having someone betray you is one of the worst feelings in the world. The feelings of anger, resentment, and pain can consume you for months or even years. What's worse than these feelings are the invisible scars that, if you're not careful, have the potential to poison all areas of your life.

Whilst my first business was booming, I took on a family member as an employee. I trusted him and felt proud that I could provide a great career for him. Six months before my business went bust, he resigned and opened a similar business to the one I had trained him in! You may be thinking, *Well, that wasn't very nice*. I agree, but it was what happened next that hurt the most. He then took a lot of money that was not his – from my customers! As you can imagine, this contributed to me losing a lot of trust in myself for my poor judgement, and in him for the betrayal. I can't deny that in that moment I was angry and upset, but it came to a point where I had to learn from my mistake of not having stronger boundaries, and I let it go.

Is it possible to learn to trust again? Absolutely. But it starts with you. Before you start to rebuild your trust in others, you need to rebuild your trust in yourself. Make decisions; keep promises; follow through with your actions; implement boundaries in your business from the beginning; have contracts in place. And if something doesn't go to plan, learn from your mistakes but do not blame yourself.

By starting to say 'yes' to yourself, you will feel a shift in your energy. Trust that every decision you make, good or bad, will still lead you to the right destination. Here's a gentle reminder that you don't have to have it all figured out, and here is also the permission to begin to trust yourself from today.

It's not essential, but you may want to buy a new T-shirt that says, 'I trust myself!' ☺

Secret #7

The Freepreneur overcomes Impostor Syndrome

Be honest with me: how many of these questions have entered your mind? 'Is anyone going to take me seriously as a business owner? Who am I to become a successful entrepreneur? Do I have enough experience? Will I be perceived as an expert in my field? What if I get found out and people think I'm a fraud?'

Some of them? Or perhaps all of them?

Let's have a look at the definition of Impostor Syndrome:

Impostor syndrome is a psychological pattern in which one doubts one's accomplishments and has a persistent internalised fear of being exposed as a 'fraud'. – Wikipedia

I have directly worked with hundreds of entrepreneurs, and I have never met a single one has hasn't suffered from this fear at one time or another in one form or another (yes, myself included!). One of the problems is that you aren't able to recognise your own achievements. You are constantly telling yourself that you will be successful once you've achieved your next goal. You achieve the goal and you then tell yourself you'll feel successful when you achieve the next goal… and so on.

It has also been linked to perfectionism. You fear being judged, and make up stories in your mind such as nobody would want to work with you if they knew you'd only been in business for two months, or nobody would want to work with you if they knew that you don't have specific qualifications in your field of expertise. Tell me this: if you're feeling thirsty and purchase a bottle of water, would it bother you if the company had been in business for two days or two decades? Would it bother you if the owner had left school at the age of 16, or had studied at the top university in the world and was the proud owner of three degrees?

I'm guessing you have never asked these questions. By drinking the water, you are no longer thirsty, so your needs have been met. And it is exactly the same for your customer! Of course, there are some exceptions where proof of qualifications and licences may be required, but the majority of business owners will never be asked.

In my Freepreneur courses and in the next book, we will be exploring how you can set up a business that will always meet your customers' needs, but until then I want you to trust that as long as your product or service meets or exceeds your customers' needs, those made-up stories in your mind have no place!

To build a long-standing business, it is imperative that you ARE able to recognise your own achievements, and that you DO NOT wait for everything to be perfect before you take action. The Freepreneur celebrates their success at every step of their journey, whether that's their first order, their first review, or their first million dollars. They will make sure their work is the best it can be, but they have the attitude of 'Don't get it perfect, get it done quickly'.

This means they take consistent action, they don't procrastinate, they build momentum, and they see results! They acknowledge the results and celebrate their success, which in turn greatly reduces or completely eliminates impostor syndrome!

Be brave and take the next step now!

Secret #8

The Freepreneur embraces failure

Despite failure being a natural part of life, nobody actually wants to fail. This deep-rooted fear has the ability to paralyse entrepreneurs into persistent procrastination. What if everything goes wrong? What will everyone think of me? What if I make the wrong decision? What if I take the wrong action?

So, what if I told you that failure is not real because there is no right or wrong decision? And that every action is the perfect action? Every decision and every action will guide you in the right direction, either by teaching you how *not* to do something or how to do something better. To set up a strong and sustainable business, you need to constantly test, test, and test again!

I want you to understand that success is a failure that failed (I heard this first from Antonio Eram, a well-known Romanian entrepreneur) and of course is very rare. This means that your trip to success will look like failure, failure, failure, failure… failure… failure… success!

Technically-speaking, failure is when you set an objective and the results that occurred didn't meet that objective. When this happens, your brain automatically shouts, 'You're a failure!' which I agree doesn't feel great, especially when you are trying your best to create a better life for you and your family.

But why, or what, are you really afraid of?

Society and social media play a big role in encouraging us to portray the perfect life with no imperfections. But for the majority of people, the biggest fear of failure stems from their childhood upbringing. By wanting to receive love and attention, they would do everything they could to avoid doing anything wrong. If they did do something wrong, or they did not meet someone else's standards, they were punished – either through words, actions, or both.

The negative feelings that became associated with the fear of failure then stay with them for a long time after their childhood ends. In fact, a lot of adults choose to punish themselves for perceived failure. If you're wondering why anyone would choose to do this, have you ever tried to lose weight, not achieved the result you desired, and then binged on a load of food? In terms of running a business, the punishment can show up as self-sabotage or, more commonly, by hiding away… because if you don't take action, you can't fail. I want to flip this belief on its head and say that if you fail to take action then you will definitely fail to succeed.

Freepreneurs understand that failure is their friend (in case you were wondering, the word friend wasn't a typing error!). They know that success is rare, and that to achieve this they need to learn through failure. They take their personal emotions out of the picture and know that it's a numbers game. They are not afraid of failure. They want to fail often. In fact, failure becomes their objective! This is because they know that the quicker they fail, the quicker they will succeed.

Still not convinced? I'd like to share a story from when I started my position as a Sales Manager for a large company in Romania. It soon became apparent that my team's sales results were very low, and they were nowhere near to achieving their full potential. Why? Because everyone was afraid of failure. My strategy might have initially seemed confusing to some, but this is what I told my team: 'When you meet with your customers, I want you to fail! As soon as you have given them the proposal, leave the meeting and phone me to tell me joyfully that you achieved your goal and that you failed.'

I admit that, at first, they thought I was a little crazy, but they trusted my plan and got to work. They would then call me after the meeting to discuss how they could improve for the next time. Can you guess what happened next? They started to sell like mad, because they weren't afraid anymore.

You may be reading this thinking, *Ok, Bodo, maybe it is ok not to fear failure when you are selling FMCG* (fast moving consumer goods, in my example), *but what about when the failure is personal. Surely that is so much worse?* If I had been reading this book prior to losing everything in 2011, I would have been inclined to agree with you. I saw myself as a huge failure and believe me when I say that I did not see my situation as a step closer to success.

But after some time, I saw the bigger picture and I felt blessed for everything that had happened at the time. If not the best, it was one of the best things that happened in my life! Like my previous sales team, you may think I am little crazy, and I'm completely ok with that. Let me explain. The collapse of my entire life transformed me completely in such a way that now I am a way better human being. If this rather large wake-up call hadn't happened, I would have continued to be undeveloped emotionally, I would have continued to have poor relationships; I would have continued to be a poor leader; I would have continued to be a poor financial manager; I would have continued to be a poor parent for my children; I would have continued to be a poor child for my mother.

And maybe the biggest blessing of all, I would never have found my true soul purpose of supporting Freepreneurs with all my heart, blood, sweat, and tears. If someone had told me back then that my biggest failure would propel me to become a true leader and that I would go on to inspire millions with my story, I would have laughed – a lot!

I could not see it at the time, but everything changed because of my BIG failure! I'm not saying it's easy to pick yourself up after a big loss, but I am living proof that it's possible. Trust that every failure is taking you one step closer towards your objective. Take your own feelings out of the equation and know that failure is an everyday occurrence for all Freepreneurs.

Allow your failures to become your stepping stones to success!

Secret #9

The Freepreneur embraces success

How many times have you said that you want to make a change in your life? I'm going to use the example of wanting to workout. You know that it will feel great for your mind as well as your body, but something seems to stop you from taking action. This is because your brain thinks it will be better for your body, but your body is also your mind (Joe Dispenza explains this concept very well in his bestseller: 'Breaking The Habit of Being Yourself'). It resists, and says, 'No! I'm ok as I am. Please don't change my state of being, I'm comfortable and feel safe like this. I am absolutely ok with the current situation, let's not make any changes.' And guess what happens? You procrastinate, you postpone, and you make excuses for not achieving your desired action by telling yourself no workout = no problem.

This resistance to change works in exactly the same way when you want to achieve a business objective. Your brain starts to see new goals and opportunities that you desire, but you don't take action. Even if you manage to overcome this procrastination, the fear of success is ready and waiting to stop you in your tracks. The reason for this is due to the apprehension of the unknown.

If you achieve success, all of your body, mind, and being will transform into a different state. You will express different emotions (especially positive emotions) and you will see the world from a different perspective. Until you push past this fear and take action, your cells will remain trapped in their old negative state of being. Like it or not, they do not want to change. It's like they are on red alert, screaming, 'Warning! Warning!'

If you have never achieved success, how do you know who you will become?

If you have never achieved success, how do you know how you will feel?

If you have never achieved success, how do you know if your personal relationships will suffer?

If you have never achieved success, how do you know that you won't turn into an idiot and all of your friends abandon you, or they will only want you for your money?

It's like a stuck record that goes on and on and on…. It likes being stuck because, in its opinion, being stuck = being safe.

The Freepreneur says, *turn that bloody record off, I'm going to make my own music!* They embrace personal development and seize the opportunity to become the best version of themselves. They love the new feelings that accompany success and feel proud that they have created a new life on their terms. They trust that if they weren't an idiot before they achieved success, then they won't suddenly turn into one after! They understand that many of their friends will never understand their journey as an Freepreneur; the right ones will stay, and if others fall away, that's ok. They know that as their wealth increases it is nothing to be ashamed of, and that it gives them the power to help even more people and on a much larger scale.

Set up your business in the right way, and success is yours for the taking. Be ready to embrace this!

Secret #10

The Freepreneur refuses to play the victim role

No matter how strong your business is, there will always be times of change and uncertainty. In an ideal world, it would be great to predict what will happen at any given moment. I hate to be the one to break it to you, but we never have and never will live in an ideal world. Every business has a degree of risk and it is your responsibility to manage this. Even the thought of dealing with an unexpected crisis may bring up some feelings of anxiety, but the real test is how you, as a business owner, cope with the situation.

As I write this part of the book in March 2020, we are in the middle of the Corona virus pandemic. The ripples of destruction have only just begun but many business owners, including myself, have already been impacted by this. So now, even more than ever, I am sharing this from a place of experience, and I'd like to tell you what has happened in my business over the last two months.

I had planned to run a free start-up seminar at the start of February. Up until this point, I'd been using direct marketing in my business, but when I noticed the conversions had dropped at the end of January, I adapted my plan. I decided to go back to my love of running large in-person events and made a reservation for a seminar room that would accommodate at least

100 attendees. My existing data told me that to fill 100 seats with a conversion rate of 30% meant that I would need 300 leads from the landing page I had created.

My plan was to promote the event solely through social media adverts. Why? Because this is one of the strategies that works well nowadays, and that I teach to my students. I set up the advert with a strategic target audience and then I waited… one by one the leads started to come in. They went from 1, to 10, to 100, to 140. Just as I was about to do a happy dance to celebrate my proven strategy again, it all came to a complete standstill. Why? Because the social media platform I chose at the time had blocked my business account!

My heart sank when I saw the notification. Surely there had to be a mistake. According to their message, my advert didn't comply with their rules, and I had one chance to appeal their decision. What on earth was I going to do? There were only six days until my event, and according to my conversion rate, going ahead with 140 leads would mean that only 40 people would turn up on the day. 40 attendees weren't enough! The seminar would be delivering free content, but to make it viable I was counting on converting a percentage of the attendees onto my weekend mastery programme. The mastery programme has powerful content, but a huge part of its success is the fact that it is run as a group programme, where everyone supports each other. I needed a Plan B and I needed it fast.

Now, I know that at this stage I should have put my positive pants on and trusted that I would be able to work out a solution. However, despite many years of experience of working directly with over 1000 entrepreneurs, I will admit that I, Bodo Codreanu, am not perfect and I am still human! (Ok, I think that's enough justification; I will continue with the story now!) I was in shock after I read the message several times over, and I felt angry. How dare they block my account? I was doing my best to inspire and support thousands of business owners! Why did these things always happen to me!?

Despite feeling frustrated, I decided not to react immediately. Why? We have a saying in Romania that the night is a very good coach. So, I decided to take this advice and went to bed early, feeling quite deflated. Maybe the seminar just wasn't meant to be.

I woke up the next day with a clearer mind. I still didn't have any answers, but I was determined to find them. I re-read the message from the platform and made some assumptions as to what I could change before messaging them back sharing that I felt there had been a mistake. An automatic reply told me that I would then have to wait 48 hours for a response.

I'll be the first to admit that I like a challenge, but this was going to be cutting it fine! I began to think about other ways to share my event, and I decided that if I hadn't heard back from them within two days, I would contact influential people in my network and ask them to promote the event through their contact lists. I wrote out a list of potential people and drafted an e-mail just in case I needed it. Thankfully, I didn't need a Plan B. I was elated to receive an email from the platform to say my appeal had been successful and that my advert was up and running again. Thank goodness for that!

With only four days to go, I watched my registrations continue to increase, and the night before the seminar I had achieved over 300 leads! I ran the seminar, received incredible feedback, and exceeded the sales target I'd set myself. Now it was time for the overdue happy dance… but not for long.

I decided to run with my success, and I booked the same room to run the same seminar one month later, on the 9th of March. The amended advert was set up, the landing page was ready, and the registrations flowed in. I was finalising my preparations the night before the seminar when I heard the shock news that due to the Corona virus spreading, the Romanian Government had passed an emergency law to ban all in-person events of more than 1000 people, and for any event less than 1000 people an official authorisation certificate was needed.

After hearing that the authorities were overwhelmed by the demand for certificates, I had to make the decision to cancel my seminar only hours before it was due to start. This was far from ideal, but as a responsible business owner, I fully understand that our health is paramount. I have to admit that I was a little disappointed to hear that at 8pm on the 9th of March the government changed the rule, so that events of less than 100 people could go ahead. But as my event had been due to start at 6pm, I knew I'd made the right decision.

I understand that the government was acting in the best interest of the country, but I needed to think quickly and once again find a Plan B. Why the hurry? My weekend mastery course already had students booked, and I didn't want to receive any cancellations. I reminded myself that I had dealt with much bigger challenges this in the past, and despite feeling some apprehension I decided I would find a way.

As I always do in challenging times, I chose to ask for some advice from other business owners who have also overcome challenges. They were all very supportive, but it was my ghostwriter, Cassandra, who encouraged me to run both my free seminar and my weekend mastery course online. This is something I had been planning to do over the coming months, but I acted fast, invited all of my registered leads from the live seminar to join a closed online group, and had over 100 attendees join me for a successful online seminar where again I sold my upgraded programme! I feel proud that not only did I avoid victim mode, but I also embraced a new opportunity to expand my business where I can now reach a worldwide audience where I will also be delivering my seminars in English. Later on, I would find out that this was the best thing ever happened in my business life for a long time.

I can tell you that in the middle of a crisis, you may initially – like I did – feel like you want to run away and hide, only coming back out once everything is safe and back to normal. From the customer's perspective, it was business as normal; in February I still ran the seminar as usual, in March I moved it online. When the unexpected hits, you may feel like your world is falling apart, but it's your responsibility to do whatever it takes to pick up the pieces, manage the customer's expectations, and still deliver the promised outcome.

It's interesting that not many people will know or even admit that they have gone into victim mode. This is because they are not aware of, and do not take responsibility for, their actions. They are far too busy making up excuses and blaming everybody else but themselves. They don't want to admit that they could possibly have contributed to the problem. They are far too busy feeling sorry for themselves, and if their own pathetic pity party doesn't gain sympathy from others, they will continue to feel miserable by themselves. In their heads they are thinking, 'Poor old me, I am a helpless and powerless human being, please will someone, anyone, feel sorry for me?'

Oh, my goodness, I can feel my energy draining just writing about this scenario! Once again, this destructive negative behaviour comes back to the powerful programming from your past. As a child, it is quite normal to have a temper tantrum if you don't get your own way, but bringing this immature behaviour into adulthood, and into your business, is a big no-no.

If you have recognised any of these traits in yourself, my intention is not to make you feel bad. Please see this as a positive and, like any constructive change, it always begins with raising your self-awareness. If it makes you feel better, I will now share how I was once the perfect victim. And yes, I really loved being the victim!

When I was in the depths of depression laying on the sofa in 2011, I was having a really big pity party!

I blamed the government for changing the political party which was in charge.

I blamed my customers who hadn't paid me on time.

I blamed my landlord who blocked the entry to my business premises.

I blamed the employee who lied to me.

I blamed the bank who took back my apartments.

I blamed the leasing company who took back my cars.

And finally, I blamed the economic crisis.

As you can see, I had a very convincing victim story which I repeated to myself over and over again. It was so much easier to feel sorry for myself than to admit the cold hard truth. The truth that I was the only one to blame, for everything.

I was the one who didn't calculate the risk of the impact of the government changing. I was the one who allowed my customers to pay me at a later date, with no insurance to reduce the risk. I was the one who didn't pay my rent on time. I was the one who was mean to my employees, resulting in them having little respect for me. I was the one who was a poor financial manager. I was the one who had not built up any savings as a reserve. I was the one who was living a life of luxury and had made poor investments for the future.

Coming to this realisation didn't happen overnight and wasn't easy. I have had to make some huge shifts in my mindset to help me accept full responsibility for my actions. And this is exactly what The Freepreneur does. They take responsibility for their actions, they admit when they've made a mistake, and they certainly never feel sorry for themselves.

If something doesn't go to plan, instead of looking for sympathy and excuses, do whatever it takes to find solutions and lessons!

Secret #11

The Freepreneur is empathetic

Empathy is the ability to share someone else's feelings or experiences by imagining what it would be like to be in that person's situation. You may be wondering what empathy has got to do with becoming a Freepreneur. Let me tell you, empathy has got everything to do with becoming a Freepreneur. In fact, I believe that this is the most important skill to adopt in the business world.

Gone are the days when empathy was seen as a soft skill that you could take or leave. If you choose to ignore instead of embracing empathy, don't come crying to me and say that I didn't warn you! You may achieve some quick wins within your business, but sooner or later your kingdom will crumble. The main reason for this is that without empathy and understanding you will not build the right product or service for your ideal customer. From now on, I want you to see empathy as a business skill that will not only serve you well with your customers, suppliers, and employees, but in every area of your life.

If you have the ability to see the world through other people's eyes, you will not only have stronger and more fulfilling relationships, but you will also gain a competitive advantage in your business. Sounds good, right? When you step away from your own agenda in every marketing communication, every negotiation, and in every sales situation, and instead begin to have a deeper understanding of their pain points, needs, and desires, then invisible positive shifts will occur. Despite living in such a fast-paced world, people are longing for connection. If you can demonstrate that you truly understand how they feel now, and more importantly how they want to feel after they have interacted with you, this will always result in a win-win outcome for both parties.

When I was discussing the importance of empathy with my ghostwriter, Cassandra, she told me about a powerful example that had happened in her business just 24 hours earlier. As I mentioned whilst writing this book, we are still living through the chaos that the Corona virus has brought to the world. It has had a detrimental impact on many people's income, as well as their lives. Cassandra was two weeks into running a new group author mentoring programme where many of her clients were paying in monthly instalments. Instead of going into fear, she sent a message to her clients saying that she understood that many people's circumstances had changed, and if this had impacted their income, she didn't want them to worry. Cassandra reassured them that they were still welcome to be a part of the programme and encouraged them to reach out to her should they need to reduce their payment or to extend their payment plan. The immediate response to her post was all of her clients thanking her for her kindness.

Her expectation was to wait for the requests to arrive. Thirty minutes later, she received her first message, and she said to herself, 'Ok, here is the first client that needs help with their payments.' When she opened the message, she was shocked to see that there was no request to reduce the monthly payment; in fact, her client wanted to increase their payment! Now that, ladies and gentlemen, is what you call the empathy effect in action! Genuine empathy will be rewarded with a genuine result. This may not always happen as quickly as Cassandra's example, but trust me when I say that what goes around comes around.

When your customers feel like you see them as human beings rather than sales on your spreadsheet, your relationship with them will become closer. Not only will your sales increase but you will also see a rise in referrals and long-term customer loyalty. Happy days!

When your employees feel like you see them as human beings rather than numbers on the payroll, they will become more focused and driven. Employee engagement and productivity will increase, which means you will see an increase in staff retention and a decrease in recruitment costs.

When your suppliers feel like you see them as human beings rather than contacts on your database, you will receive a better service and see your outgoings decrease.

I know this all sounds good so far but be warned there is a dark side to empathy. There are some people who believe they are very empathetic, but what they really are is very persuasive. This behaviour may achieve a short-term sale, but it won't achieve a long-lasting relationship. It's very simple: for empathy to be effective it has to be genuine and authentic.

Empathy was a skill that I gave very little thought to prior to the collapse of my business in 2011. Why did I need to see the world from anyone else's perspective when in my mind it was me against the world? You don't need me to remind you what the outcome of my closed-minded thinking was, but I can tell you that one of my biggest mistakes was having little to no empathy for my customers, my suppliers, my landlord, my bank, my employees, or anyone else in life at that time.

I can confidently share that I have definitely learnt my lesson, and now I endeavour to demonstrate authentic empathy in all of my relationships. In my seminars I take pride in learning about my students and I am available to help them with their needs, wants, and desires. In doing so, I have been able to provide a better service, and created better products which in turn created better results, better retention, and an increase in referrals.

Something else I have seen an increase in is collaboration opportunities. Collaborations will only be successful if the people within them are speaking the same language, and this is where empathy comes into play. And let me tell you a little secret: the more empathy you deploy, the more sensitive you become to people's needs, and the higher your desire becomes to truly help others. This is where the Law of Attraction comes into place. The more you give, the more you get.

So, to conclude, the healthier your relationships are the healthier your business will be. But the best side effect of all is the impact that empathy will have on your own personal state of being.

As your empathy increases so will your own fulfilment and happiness!

Secret #12

The Freepreneur has an abundance mindset

Your attitude toward scarcity and abundance will greatly influence your success as an entrepreneur. Stephen Covey explains these concepts beautifully in his classic book, *The 7 Habits of Highly Effective People*. He writes:

"Most people are deeply scripted in what I call the Scarcity Mentality. They see life as having only so much, as though there were only one pie out there. And if someone were to get a big piece of the pie, it would mean less for everybody else.

The Scarcity Mentality is the zero-sum paradigm of life. People with a Scarcity Mentality have a very difficult time-sharing recognition and credit, power or profit—even with those who help in the production. They also have a hard time being genuinely happy for the success of other people.

The Abundance Mentality, on the other hand, flows out of a deep inner sense of personal worth or security. It is the paradigm that there is plenty out there and enough to spare for everybody. It results in the sharing of prestige, recognition, profits and decision-making. It opens possibilities, options, alternatives and creativity."

I love the concept of having enough pie to go around, but I also have my own concept that relates more specifically to businesses. Every business needs a balance of cashflow to be able to survive and thrive;

there needs to be a regular flow of money coming in and there needs to be a regular flow of money going out. I teach the students in my Freepreneur courses that they are all part of a worldwide cash flow machine. This infrastructure, held together by metaphorical money pipes, has already been in place for thousands of years. You can be part of this, all you need to do is plug your business money pipes into the worldwide money pipes system and enjoy the flow.

When you join the pipeline with an abundance mindset, the cash flow continues, money in, money out, money in, money out… When you join the pipeline with a scarcity mindset, you become a stagnant cork that stops the flow! Why is this? If you are a tight arse that negotiates discounts on every single deal, if you are the customer that always pays your bills late, or you are the business owner that resents giving your time or resources to help others, you clog up the pipe and block the flow of (your) abundance. On the other hand, if you pay your bills on time and with gratitude, trust that there is plenty of money for everyone whilst generously giving your time, energy, and resources to others, your cash will keep flowing and your business will keep growing! (Yes, I like rhyming!)

Developing an abundance mindset is something that I have worked on for many years and is a continual work in progress. Every month I take pride in donating a percentage of my time to coach people who are not in a financial position to pay the higher rates that my client base pays. Over the years as an entrepreneur I have received gifts of time from my mentors, and it's important for me to give back. I trust in karma and know that everything I give out to the worldwide economic pipeline will be returned back to me in one way or another.

Whilst some established businesses will plug into the pipeline by donating a sum of money to a designated charity, there are other ways that you can be a good giver, even if you're just starting out. You can give your undivided attention to anyone in your network. If you are speaking to them in person, are you maintaining eye contact or are you looking over their shoulder wondering who to speak to next? If you are on a phone or video call, are you actively listening or is your mind distracted whilst you are constantly checking your notifications? You may wonder what difference this may make, but it all comes back to energy. It may not be seen but it can be felt.

Much as giving is important, The Freepreneur is also an excellent receiver. They graciously receive new clients as well as payments for their goods and services. They love receiving compliments and will thank the giver, knowing that saying, 'Thank you' is enough. Is this something that you find challenging? It can take practice, but I want you to notice the difference in the energy next time you receive a compliment and simply smile and say thank you. The Universe will reward you with even more, so enjoy!

I feel it's also important to mention that The Freepreneur knows their value and isn't afraid to charge and receive payment for this. One of my students, Andrei, joined my courses with the inspired idea to design and develop a premium clothing line for doctors' uniforms. He had discovered that many doctors and consultants would like to wear a medical gown that is of high quality and has the option to be personalised and made to stand out from their colleagues, whilst still being in keeping with their required uniform.

As part of my training, I encourage my students to delve deeply into not only the practical needs of their clients, but also their emotional traits. What Andrei found on completing his research was that his ideal client craved attention from others and sought external validation through possessions. Initially, this caused him a block, which he discussed during our weekly class. He asked if it was fair to create and charge these clients for a premium product in what could be perceived as taking advantage of one of their potential emotional problems.

My reply? Was it fair *not* to create this product when there appeared to be a demand? Think about it for a moment. This is exactly what a Freepreneur does; they create and charge for an effective solution to resolve their clients' problems! Almost everything that you have ever bought is because you wanted it to solve a problem. And believe me, if you don't run with a business opportunity to help solve other people's problems, then someone else will! With this doctor in mind, there will also be entrepreneurs who are bringing designer watches, pens, and notebooks, to the market which will also have a premium look, feel, and price. They take the rightful place in the worldwide money pipeline.

The secret to keeping a constant flow in the money pipeline is having balance. The Freepreneur is a great giver as well as a great receiver. If you stop giving or receiving, you will become the cork in the money pipeline that flows around the entire economy.

Don't be the cork! Enjoy, trust, and let the cash flow to let your business grow!

Secret #13

The Freepreneur embraces feedback

You are the expert. You are respected by many people. You have all the answers, don't you? If you think that embracing feedback doesn't apply to you, then I'd encourage you to gently place your ego to one side and read this section of the book at least twice! I agree that you are the expert and I'm sure that you are respected by many people for your knowledge and expertise, but the Freepreneur knows that this on its own is not enough. Receiving feedback is a vital part of your ongoing development, and I actively encourage you to constantly look for ways to embrace this.

There are several types of feedback that you may receive in your business. Before I continue, I'd like to share at this point that I don't believe in the perception of feedback being either positive or negative; I like to think that all feedback is important and constructive information.

Feedback from your clients

Whether this is prompted or unprompted, cherish your customer's voice and understand that the more feedback you receive the more clarity you will gain. It helps you to clarify the customer's expectations as well as helping your customer to feel like their opinion is important. By asking them to complete a simple survey, to provide a business review, or by having an open and honest conversation, it gives you the chance to solve any present problems as well as the opportunity to fulfil any of their future needs. The more time you spend with your customers, the better your products and services will be. If you don't listen and act on this invaluable source of information, then be warned that your competition will!

Feedback from your Key Performance Indicators, Objectives and Key Results

As the old saying goes, 'if it's not measured then it can't be improved'. What is the point of setting business goals if you're not analysing the results and comparing these with your objectives? It's imperative to review your company sales feedback on a regular basis. This will put you in a position of control, to be proactive rather than reactive with important decisions that arise as result of this. If you fail to measure, analyse, and gain feedback, you may as well run your business wearing a blindfold! You will not be in a position to see what is working well, what isn't working well, and what needs to be changed.

Feedback from your business network

Whether this is from your coach, mentor, business peers, or colleagues, I can guarantee that at some point you will receive feedback that is vital to help you with your own personal development. From experience, I understand that this isn't always a skill that comes naturally. Even with the best will in the world, receiving feedback can trigger your defence mechanism to kick in, which places a big blame barrier around you to deflect anything that could be deemed as negative. Remember how I said that there is no such thing as negative feedback? This is the time to really reinforce this. Each and every one of us sees life through our own unique life lens. There are thousands of different reasons why someone may have a different perspective to you, and that's ok.

If you feel your blame barrier being activated, take a deep breath and remember that there are very few people that are deliberately trying to upset you with their feedback. The majority of the time they want to help you to become the best version of yourself, and they have identified something that you aren't able to see through your own life lens. When you understand that personal feedback is a gift to be lovingly accepted and not rejected, you will discover so much more about yourself than you could ever learn from a book or a business seminar. Yes, it may take some practice, and that's ok, but by far the best way to accept feedback is to simply thank the person for sharing. That's it: no blame, justification, or argument needs to follow.

After the conversation, take some time to reflect on what was said, and think about how you could make any positive changes to your behaviour. This personal ownership takes a lot of strength, combined with deep emotional maturity, but once you master this skill your personal growth as well as your relationships, in business and in your personal life, will flourish.

Feedback from your conversations

Every time you have a conversation, you are doing so to convey a message. I'm sure I'm not the only one who has had a genuine misunderstanding arise for no other reason than the other person thought I meant one thing when I actually meant something else. This doesn't mean that they were right, and I was wrong, or vice versa. We are all human, and from time to time miscommunication happens. But wouldn't you agree that business and life run so much smoother with clear communication?

The simple way to know whether your message has been heard, and more importantly understood, is by asking for feedback. This could be as simple as asking, 'Does that make sense?' or 'Have I explained that clearly?' or 'Is there anything else you'd like to know?' This can save valuable time and money, especially if there are actions to be followed up from your conversations.

Not asking for feedback across your business could be compared to sailing across the ocean without using a compass. A compass is an essential way to receive feedback on where you are on your journey at any given moment. By checking it on a regular basis, you will know if you are on or, more importantly, off track. Even if you have to readjust your sails or divert in a different direction, you will be guaranteed to reach your desired destination in a much shorter time.

Get ready to set your sails for success! Grab your compass and embrace all feedback!

Secret #14

The Freepreneur is in love with solving customers' problems

I'm so in love with my ideas, products, and services said no Freepreneur ever! You may be wondering if I've made a mistake. Surely you have to be in love with your ideas, products, and services, right? Wrong!

Let's go back to basics. The majority of inspiring entrepreneurs are head over heels in love with their brand-new magical idea that they hope will change the world. They keep it all to themselves, not daring to tell anyone else in case their idea is stolen, and their magical dream slips away quicker than you can say abracadabra! They hide away, keeping their beloved idea close to their heart, whilst they imagine running a successful business. They imagine their customers paying them so that they can then imagine living their successful business life.

When they do finally step out of their dream world, there is usually one of two outcomes: they either find out that their magnificent idea has already been brought to life, or they have acquired 327 special certifications, 17 medals for their invention, and craploads of needless debt! I think you'll agree that neither outcome is ideal. They may have succeeded in inventing a product or service that they thought the world needed, but they haven't succeeded in making an impact or making the world a better place. Why?

Because they forgot to add the missing ingredient for true success – fast client feedback!

You will now have a much greater awareness of client feedback, having just read Secret #13, but I want to reiterate its importance, right from the very start of your journey. I have seen many entrepreneurs make the mistake of going into full-on inventor mode, and then asking for feedback after their product or service has been created. I'm sorry to be the bearer of bad news, but this will rarely work. It is too little too late. The consequences will be a lot of wasted time, energy, and money, not to mention a huge dent to your self-confidence.

I can hear your brain spinning as you try to get your head around this new concept, and I wouldn't blame you for wanting to question this theory. Surely the best businesses in the world all start with an amazing idea that ends up becoming an incredible customer solution!? I agree that every successful business started with an idea, but it's what you do with that idea that is either the key to your success or the key to your failure. To explain further, I want to look at the definition of these words:

Invent: To create or design (something that has not existed before).

Innovate: To make changes in something established, especially by introducing new methods, ideas, or products.

I now want to introduce you to two of my imaginary friends – John and Joanna. (Please don't worry, my imaginary friends are just for the purpose of the book!)

John spends time, money, and energy on inventing a product that he loves. He keeps his ideas close to his heart but chooses to gently massage his ego by seeking feedback from his mum, girlfriend, and Dave who lives down the road. John waits until he has found what he thinks is the perfect solution before finally sharing his magnificent idea with the real world and attempts to make sales.

Joanna has the idea to invent a new product, but she keeps her ego in check and remains detached. Before taking any further action on her idea, she seeks her potential customers' insights and feedback to gauge whether her idea will be successful in solving her customers' problems. She then uses this valuable feedback to innovate her original idea before she commits her time, money, and energy on innovating the final solution, that will be sold before it is ready to bring to the market.

Based on these examples, who do you feel is the Freepreneur? If you guessed Joanna, then take a moment to give yourself a real (or imaginary) pat on the back and then I'll continue. Can you see how Joanna's logic is going to bring her better results? As a side note, I used the example of creating a product, but this strategy is relevant whether you are creating a product, a service, or if your business will be in commerce.

I teach this technique of how to turn an idea into a paying customer in the Freepreneur courses. I encourage my students to focus purely on the customers' challenges, and to fall in love with solving customers' problems instead of falling in love with what they believe is a magical solution. Once they have grasped this shift in their mindset, that's when the real magic happens. They begin to sell their products and services with ease. Sometimes from a simple piece of paper, sometimes from a simple landing page, and sometimes from a simple demo video. If you're wondering if someone would really spend their hard-earned cash and make a purchase from a piece of paper, just remember that tens of thousands of new build houses are sold in this way every year when the developers are selling the plots off-plan.

Now you understand that a solution is only brought to the market after receiving valuable customer feedback, you may be wondering if it is now ok to fall in love with your new product or service. No! Not now. Not ever! There are two reasons for this.

The first is that you should never become attached to your products or services because they are not yours, they are your customers'. If you become attached, then you will start to involve emotion in what should remain as strategic decisions to keep or discard them, according to how well they are performing.

The second reason is that markets are constantly changing, your customers' behaviours are constantly changing, and your customers' desires are constantly changing, not to mention that you are not the only one in the market – your competitors will also be constantly adapting.

Even though you have received customer feedback, your work is never done. Do not – I repeat, do not – get complacent and put your business blinkers on. It is your job to be the entire research and development department, and it is your job to constantly be striving to solve the customers' problems.

How do you do this? By always asking for feedback, and by spending quality time with your customers. I learnt this valuable lesson first-hand when I studied for my Executive MBA at Cotrugli Business School, where I researched how Procter and Gamble was such a successful business. They sell a vast range of fast-moving household products. To gain a crystal-clear understanding of their customers' problems, they were known to actually spend time in their customers' houses! Yes, you read that right. Even the CEO has been known to take part in this ingenious idea, to ensure they stayed ahead of the competition by knowing their customers' challenges better than anyone else.

Moreover, I worked for the Procter & Gamble division in the biggest sales company in Romania, and even though it wasn't part of my role to stay in the customers' houses, on many occasions I spent hundreds of hours in front of the shelves inside the stores where the products were sold, talking, interacting, and asking questions to the customers who were interested in our products. What were they looking for? What did they love about the product?

Was the packaging important to them? Were they able to find all of the information on the label? Were they happy with the price? These were simple questions that gave invaluable answers. Believe me when I say that not many business owners think about, let alone implement, this strategy of making it their duty to put their customers' problems first.

At the opposite end of the scale, the business owners that care more about massaging their own ego rather than focusing on customers' problems are more likely to be found having a full-on pity party when they see a drop in revenue. It couldn't possibly be their fault, could it? Surely the customer has to be blamed for not purchasing the product. They don't know what they're missing out on!

Would you agree that this is not a productive way to build a successful business? Anyone else smell a victim? The Freepreneur takes full responsibility for their customers' happiness and for letting nothing come between them and finding out and loving their customers' problems now, and in the future.

Take the full responsibility and always solve your ideal customer's problem!

Secret #15

The Freepreneur fulfils their dream(s)

Giving up on your dream is not an option. I know that starting and growing a business is not easy, but quitting one is. There may be many times when you feel like the pressure and overwhelm has got too much and you feel like calling it a day. Believe it or not, one of the main reasons that this downwards spiral can escalate out of control is due to your own voice. Yes, really! I'm not talking about the voice that comes out of your mouth; I'm talking about the voice that torments you in your head and tells you that maybe this business isn't such a good idea after all, that you haven't got what it takes, and that you're never going to make it.

Another reason for wanting to give up are the voices from other people, whether that's your family, friends, or colleagues. There will always be someone who would prefer to see you playing small and not striving for your dreams. There will be some people who will give you their full-on support, but it's sad to say that many people will choose to give you full-on crap! They may think that you're crazy for wanting to change your life and make a difference in the world.

My advice? Dig deeper, learn more, grow more, implement all of the beliefs you've just read, do it anyway, and prove them wrong. No matter whether it's your own voice or the voice of others, my advice is still the same: hold your dream(s) close to your heart and do not quit.

You now know the story about how I was determined to pick up the pieces of my life when I was 31, but my relentless determination started a long time before that. When I was 12 years old, my passion for music was ignited. I loved nothing more than to listen to my radio all day and all night; in fact, it wasn't unusual for me to wake up in the morning with the tunes still playing. It was at this time that I decided that when I grew up my dream was to become a radio star. I would close my eyes, listen to the music, and visualise how it would feel to hear my voice beaming down the radio waves.

When I was 14 – four years after the communism had ended in Romania – I started at a new technical high school, where one of the older students had the idea of creating an internal radio station where music and announcements would be played in between our lessons. Oh, my goodness, this was it. This was my moment; my chance to move a step closer towards my big dream.

I was so excited to be invited to an interview, followed by a trial to show them just how good I was. I had every faith that I would get chosen. How could they refuse a walking, talking musical encyclopaedia aka DJ Bodo?

Have you ever had a time in your life when one moment you feel like you could take over the world, and the next moment your world has collapsed around your feet? You guessed it; I didn't get chosen. I was told that I didn't have what it takes, that I would never be any good, and that I should leave and go home. My heart felt like it had been ripped out and stamped on. What was wrong with me? Why wasn't I good enough? I had tried my best, but it wasn't enough.

I went home that day feeling sad and empty. I didn't fall asleep with the radio on that night, as it was a painful reminder of what I had lost. As I mentioned earlier, we have the saying in Romania that the night is a good coach and I trust it to be true, as the next day I woke up with a spring in my step. Nobody had the right to steal my dream. I'm a very competitive person, and for me there was only one place – and that was the first place. No, I didn't get chosen for the school radio station, but I was still determined to achieve my dream. I was going to prove them wrong. I felt more motivated than ever and decided that I didn't just want to be an ordinary radio star; I wanted to be the best radio presenter in my county, if not the whole damn country!

I had to use all of my willpower to keep motivated because, to make matters worse, one of the successful DJ's to be chosen out of ten competitors was my classmate that I sat next to every single day for four long years. So, every day I was reminded of my failure and his success by hearing his voice beaming out over the school airwaves. He occasionally let me have a turn in the studio in exchange for completing his homework, but for me it was never enough.

I finished high school when I was 18 and heard that the biggest radio station in the county was recruiting for a new presenter. This was almost unheard of, but apparently a lot of the presenters had left, and they were looking for a replacement DJ as soon as possible. Before you could say 'DJ Bodo in the house!', I had applied for the position. And I was over the moon to receive a date for a live trial. I turned up for my interview, gave it my all and after only five minutes I was hired – right then and there!

After a few months of being the host for some shows where the audience was smaller, I was then entrusted with the very popular morning programmes and late-night talk shows, which attracted 60% of the entire listeners tuning in! I constantly received incredible feedback, along with a promotion to become the Technical Director. I was also asked to be the Executive Manager of the entire radio station!

You might be wondering how I went from the 14-year-old boy who had his radio dreams broken to the 18-year-old man who saw his radio dreams come true. The answer is that I never once gave up on my dream. When I woke up feeling motivated the morning after my first failed attempt, I knew that it wasn't enough to just want my dream; I needed to consistently work hard and smart towards my dream. And so, I did. I built my own amplifier, speakers, and music mixer, and DJ Bodo was born!

Over the next four long years, I spent at least five hours every day pretending to broadcast my very own radio show live from my bedroom. I would read out the news from the daily newspapers, play requests, and mix music for at least five hours a day. All alone in my bedroom. Some may say that I was a bit too dedicated, as I was known to miss school occasionally, due to my obsession to be the best that I could be.

As soon as I was old enough at the age of 16, I would DJ at parties, and when I turned 18 I would DJ in nightclubs. So, you could say that with over 4000 hours of practice under my belt at the time of the radio station interview, I became an 'overnight success' and achieved my goal!

As I write this book today in 2020, I am now in the eighth year of following my dream to become the greatest entrepreneurship motivator in Europe by 2025. Just like my radio dream, I am holding my vision close in my heart, and know that one day at a time, one step at a time, I will inspire a new generation of entrepreneurs. I decided to call them Freepreneurs. And in doing so, I will reach my goal.

There have been times when the voice in my head has told me to quit; there have been times when other people have laughed at me and wanted me to quit. It hasn't been easy, but I continue to follow the same cycle that I teach my students, by consistently learning, doing, receiving feedback, incorporating it, and then repeating!

I have invested heavily in mentors, coaches, personal development, therapy, and training. As you know, I also worked as an employee for four years to learn more skills and to build up some more financial resources, before diving back into the entrepreneurial world in 2017. Even while I was working full time, I still spent time on my business in my 'spare' time. I would allocate time to spend with my family, but no matter what was happening in my life, I would always make time in the evenings and weekends to study my MBA, and to travel around Europe to attend numerous training courses as I constantly learned, researched, and tested the systems, strategies, and tools that I now teach.

They say that one of the biggest regrets of the dying is that they didn't follow their dreams and desires when they had the time in their life. Make a promise to yourself now that you will not have that same regret. No, it's not easy. Yes, there will be obstacles. But trust that one day at a time, one step at a time, you too will reach your goal.

If you feel worried about the financial pressure of not having a regular income, my advice is to have a least six – ideally 12 – months' worth of money saved to cover your household bills. If this isn't possible, then just like I did, start by investing a small amount of time and money in your business on the side; even ten minutes and $3 per day could be enough to get started.

As your journey evolves, know that it is normal to have some setbacks. Whether it's your first unhappy customer or the bank manager not agreeing to lend you money, dig deep and trust that you have everything it takes to overcome any obstacle. The real price that you will pay for giving up is not financial. The feeling of letting yourself down and not fulfilling your purpose will stay with you for a long time after deciding that you've had enough.

I understand how challenging this journey can be, but I also know how rewarding it can be. And I want you to feel the satisfaction of waking up every day and loving every moment of serving your customers, whilst living a successful business life on your terms.

If I can do it, then you can, too. Promise me that you too will hold your vision close to your heart and that you will…

Never, ever give up!

Secret #16

The Freepreneur is laser-focused

Have you ever got to the end of the week and wondered where the time has gone? One week can roll into one month when you are feeling disheartened that your 'to do' list still has a lot of items 'to do'! You may temporarily slip into victim mode as you declare that there is not enough time in the day. But if you're honest with yourself, you know that everyone has the same 24 hours in the day, and it's what you do – or what you don't do – that makes them count.

Have you ever quickly logged onto your social media account to gently ease yourself into your working day? Perhaps you have the intention of making a post or setting up an advert, but before you know it, you're watching a motivational video that your friend shared. Then you've wished three random people (you've never met) Happy Birthday, then you've registered for another free life-changing webinar, before feeling very important as you reply to four personal messages, made a quick post about what you're having for lunch, before scrolling through your newsfeed to see what everyone else had for lunch, watched the webinar, responded to a few comments, scrolled a bit more… and suddenly the day is almost over and you still didn't set up the advert!

Ok, so I may have slightly exaggerated in this example, but you get the picture. If you don't have your business blinkers firmly on, you will be distracted in your everyday actions which leads to not progressing your business goals.

Another example is going to the supermarket without a shopping list, especially when you're hungry – you're asking for trouble! Chances are you will end up buying all of the bright and shiny offers that you can't live without, only to get home to find that you have a bag full of wine, chocolate, and popcorn, but nothing to eat for dinner! You will have wasted time and money due to your lack of planning and not focusing on what matters, despite telling yourself that this time will be different, and you will only buy what you need! It never works. If you're not focused on your objective, you will be multi-tasking, which is never a recipe for success – even with wine, chocolate, and popcorn!

The Freepreneur does not believe in multitasking. They are clear on their mission and they are clear on the steps they need to take to keep moving closer to achieving their mission. They also start their week with a to do list, but instead of wasting time on social media they will have a clear plan which they will stick to.

Only once they have made good progress will they pass time on social media. They are disciplined and they are not easily distracted, and this laser-focused mindset applies to all areas of their life. They value their work/life balance, have respectful boundaries, and want to give their full focus and energy to the important relationships. This means if they are on a phone call, they are not also responding to their messages, or if they are at the dinner table, they are not also checking their e-mails.

If you try to constantly juggle your work and home life, the very simple fact is that you will either mess up your relationships, your business, or both! I understand that working for yourself can be stressful and that you want to be the best you can be, but I promise you that success doesn't taste so sweet if you lose everyone you love along the way. If you need to delegate or outsource some work, this is a great way to ease some pressure. If you need to have a work and family schedule, then put this in place.

I am often asked when the right time is to set up a second or multiple businesses. My answer is when you are solving your customers' problems, meeting your objectives, have a sustainable business system (including people, robots and tools), and making a profit.

Do not, I repeat, do not be tempted to set up 15 businesses at the same time. Or just because your first business hasn't made a profit immediately, don't go chasing the next shiny opportunity. Growing a successful business takes time, patience, and a laser-focused mindset. It is never a sprint but a marathon.

It's worth mentioning that having a laser-focused mindset with clearer boundaries will also increase your overall emotional wellbeing. By having a defined routine in place, you will feel less overwhelmed, and the chances are you will sleep better and wake up feeling like you're ready to take over the world. You have to wake up every day feeling motivated and energised with that roaring fire in your soul.

Build a laser-focused mission, a strong and sustainable business, and a step-by-step simple implementation strategy!

Secret #17

The Freepreneur understands how to manage risk

Risk management is when a business proactively identifies, assesses, and takes action on any risks that could potentially affect it trading. I'm aware that even reading the word 'risk' may trigger feelings of anxiety and has been known to set some entrepreneurs into a panic. They initially don't want to think about any threats to their business, let alone manage them. If they had it their way, they would dive straight in at the deep end, serving their clients without investing the invaluable time required to proactively protect their second most valuable asset – their business. I say second most valuable, as I believe our first most valuable asset is our health. If you have ever fallen into the 'risk management = too much hassle' category, I want you to begin to take care of your business in the same way that you take care of your health and your life!

From a young age, you learnt how to protect yourself, how not to poison yourself, and how not to expose yourself to any harmful risks. I know that you applied this knowledge and that you were successful in your mission, because you are here right now reading these words! In the same way, I'm asking you to transfer this knowledge into how you manage your business and to see it as a real-life being that needs protecting.

Does this seem like a strange concept? Think about it like this: there are some viruses that can unexpectedly attack your immune system, and there are some other diseases that are within us that we need to receive tests for. Even if the test is negative, your doctor may give you advice on how to maintain your health so that your symptoms don't become worse. This could be compared to unexpected business risks, such as a financial crisis, a workforce crisis, a supplier crisis, a health crisis, a sales crisis, or a cash flow crisis. They may not be completely unavoidable, but by investing in your own business doctor – aka a mentor, coach, consultant, accountant, or financial adviser – they can help to provide your business with a health check-up and guidance, which can help you to put plans in place to reduce or prevent the risk.

As I previously mentioned, I am writing this book in 2020 when the global Corona virus pandemic is in full force. Hundreds of thousands of businesses have gone bust in a matter of days. Having lost my first business, I will be the first to empathise with how the business owners must feel after such a sudden loss, but I'm going to put my assertive head on and give this to you straight. Having heard many business owners saying that it's not their fault and that's the Corona virus that has ruined their company, I would ask them these questions to help them to evaluate what really went wrong:

Where was your safety savings account, and why wasn't there enough money in there to keep your business afloat during this unforeseen time? Did you constantly monitor the cash flow in your businesses? Were you selling your products and services on a deferred payment plan? If you were, did you have an effective contract in place? Did you know what your break-even point was so that you could quickly react to the loss of revenue and reduce your fixed costs? Did you have a different sales/income strategy in place to increase your income in the unlikely event that your revenue dropped? If you had employed staff, did you plan in advance so that they could continue to work autonomously? Did you have back-up scenarios so that you can continue to trade in an emergency?

If your business was affected by the Corona virus, you may be feeling temped to throw your book across the room right now! I fully understand that some businesses could not have been saved, but I am sharing some tough love here so that your current or future business never has to experience this upsetting upheaval ever again. Of course, I'm not saying that you could have predicted the massive ripples of destruction that have been felt across the world, but by building some risk-absorbing pillars, your empire might wobble in a crisis but it's unlikely to collapse and fall.

The Freepreneur understands that from the very beginning of their business it is imperative to have solid foundations. That includes working with only ideal customers, working with ideal suppliers, working with ideal collaborators, ideal employees, ideal processes, an ideal marketing strategy, as well as an ideal branding and sales process.

I know we don't live in an ideal world, but when you have completed a thorough analysis of your business, you may be surprised at how you can protect your business through setting up risk management procedures and comprehensive contracts and insurance. Another way to minimise risk is to have different customer segments in different regions. I would also encourage you to have different income streams for your business, along with different sales strategies from different marketing channels – in other words, don't put all of your business eggs in one basket!

It would be impossible to have everything in place from day one, but it is possible to have strong contracts and terms and conditions set up before you make your first sale. It is also possible to open a safety savings account, and to transfer into this account a percentage of your first invoice and from every sale thereon. One of the main benefits of having an effective risk management system is that once it's in place, you can relax and enjoy running your business with the peace of mind that you are protected. Exactly like in your personal life.

I teach the students in my Freepreneur courses how to give themselves peace of mind by conducting a risk analysis of their business. Using the results from this exercise, they can then prepare and plan for any unexpected events or circumstances which are out of their control.

One of my most successful clients, Georgiana Voinea, owns a consultancy business which specialises in environmental protection and waste management services for companies. When she set her business up, Georgiana didn't make her first sale until she had consulted her lawyer to create a bespoke set of terms and conditions for her clients. Over eight years later, she still follows this practice, as well as regularly transferring money into both her business and personal safety savings account.

On my recommendation, in 2019 she also set up a separate bank account for her business tax. This was to enable her to manage her cash flow even more effectively. How does this work? From every payment received, she transfers a percentage into this account, so that she will have the money available when the monthly tax payment is due. This has made the payment of tax almost effortless. How many entrepreneurs can say that!?

As her business has grown, Georgiana has continually invested time, energy, and money in coaching and consultancy, as well as investing in processes and tools, digital presence, and her personal brand. She is also constantly investing in developing new and improved products and services. Georgiana's work has reduced due to the Corona virus, but she does not need to panic due to the strong pillars that she set up for herself and her business. Not only has she had the money to pay her taxes when most entrepreneurs are asking the state for a delayed payment, but she also has money in her business and personal savings account to keep her business alive.

She will definitely survive through this time of change, as her business was prepared for the unexpected. But moreover, she is spending her time in lockdown to invest in new products and services to further develop her business during and immediately after the crisis. Can you imagine the peace of mind she now feels, knowing that her business will see accelerated growth as soon as the crisis ends? In comparison, many of her competitors failed to manage the risk, and some will be closing or reducing their workforce. They weren't prepared for the unexpected. Georgiana 1; Competitors 0! I am proud to be supporting her at this time to continue to develop her business strategy and to share this success with you.

If you have been inspired by Georgiana's example, my advice is not to hesitate to put your own pillars in place. Once your pillars are in place, I recommend updating your policies and procedures on a regular basis, in the same way that you would take your body to the doctors for a check-up. Trust me when I say that if you take your business – or your health – for granted, you will pay for it later. Prevention really does pay off.

The bad news is that there are no guarantees in business or in life. But without an effective risk management strategy, I can guarantee that unexpected risks can cost you not only a lot of money but, worst case scenario, could cause your business to permanently close. I don't have any regrets in my past, but I have wondered how different things might have been if I'd had a mentor for risk management before 2011 – one who had shared the importance of protecting everything that I had worked so hard to build.

Manage risks effectively and you will have the best chance of not only surviving, but thriving, throughout times of uncertainty!

Secret #18

The Freepreneur supports their body, mind, and soul

You have just read the heading for Secret #18 and wondered if you were still reading *Secrets of the Freepreneur*! Yes, you are, and I'm serious when I say that all three areas of support are vitally important.

Your business, and your success, starts with you. Period.

I will admit that if someone had shared this information with me at the beginning of my entrepreneurial journey, I would have laughed, a lot! But I will also admit that I was not laughing when time and time again I was hitting metaphorical brick walls in my business and personal life, because I was too closed-minded to admit that anything other than sales and strategy was going to bring success.

Yes, I'd had material success in business, but I had never felt truly complete and fulfilled as a person. Well, not until I had embraced and integrated all three elements of support into my life. That's when the magic happened for me, so let me save you a lot of time and effort by sharing that the same is applicable to you.

Let's go back to those categories of support. I want to share with you the different types of support available and the huge benefits they will bring to your business, as well as to your personal life.

Body support

If you're anything like I was in the past, you might have been guilty of taking your body for granted – until you feel pain or discomfort, and then you feel angry and frustrated and would do anything to return to a state of feeling normal. Our health is everything. And if we choose to neglect instead of nourishing it, we are the ones who will suffer in the long run.

I understand that preparing green smoothies, eating quinoa, and running marathons, aren't everyone's cup of (green!) tea, but making small changes like decreasing caffeine and alcohol, reducing or eliminating sugar, dairy, and meat, and increasing fruit, vegetables, and water, can all make a big difference. Having a healthy lifestyle and providing your body with good nutrition, plenty of rest, and regular exercise, will all help your physical health, which in turn will increase your daily productivity.

Mind Support

Having read part one, you will have a deeper understanding of why your mindset and beliefs play such an important role in your business. Never underestimate the importance of healthy thinking and the knock-on effect this will have on making good decisions. Freepreneurs make supporting their mind a priority, as they understand this will help them to be more organised and to feel less stressed. They also know that when challenges and obstacles do occur, they will be able to cope so much better, due to having strategies to help them feel calm and back in control. This means they will be able to act rationally, instead of overacting and potentially making the situation worse.

You will need to constantly seek and implement new ways to support your conscious mind, through learning business and knowledge, as well as supporting your subconscious mind with a regular meditation practice. If you think that means meditating once a month when you feel stressed, think again!

If you are wondering where you will find the time to develop these new habits, I recommend having a very honest look at the distractions in your life. *What distractions?* I hear you cry! Let me ask you this: have you ever monitored how much time you waste on social media each day? You might be convincing yourself that you are 'working', but we both know that even with the best will in the world we can waste a lot of time that could be spent on feeding your profits instead of feeding your dopamine levels! Perhaps you have the willpower to only log on to make a post or to contribute to a few key groups, or maybe you need to set a daily time limit on your phone that will notify you when you have exceeded this.

Just like any new habit, it may feel strange at first. And I can tell you from experience that your mind will come up with many different reasons (aka excuses) as to why it doesn't want to change. But trust me, give it time and it will be worth it.

Soul support

Soul support means taking complete responsibility for your emotional and spiritual development. What has soul support got to do with running a business? Everything. Yes, that's right. Like it or not, we all have a past. And, like it or not, we all have wounds from our past. Every single person, event, or experience has left us with an invisible residue of positive and negative emotions. The positive ones aren't a problem, but the irony is that these are the ones we more often than not forget about. It's the negative ones that we carry around day in, day out, and if we're not careful they will not only sabotage our business, but also our lives.

One of the biggest challenges with healing wounds from your past is that they have been carefully hidden away whilst you have moved forward with your life. A lot of the time the wounds go unnoticed or they become integrated into the way you behave, so that you think this behaviour is just the way you are. Many people, including myself, have repeated destructive behavioural patterns time and time again, often blaming other people or situations for negative outcomes when actually the real reason was due to hidden, unhealed wounds.

When your rational mind rules you, it also has the power to ruin you. I want you to know that every living person has a past, and everyone has made 'mistakes'. I also want you to know that more often than not there is only so much 'on the surface' healing that we can do. To truly heal these wounds, we need to go deeper. There is not a 'one size fits all' solution here; there are many different types of healing, including taking part in spiritual practices. If you set the intention that you are ready to begin your healing journey, more often than not the Universe will guide you in the right direction. It takes a lot of courage, not to mention patience, to go deeper within your soul and to bring these shadows into the light.

Seeking emotional or spiritual support does not mean that you are weak. It means that you are strong and self-aware enough to face the shadows of yourself that, if left in the dark, can destroy your light. Introducing emotional and spiritual support into your life will more than likely cause a positive ripple effect back into your body and mind support. If you can begin to love yourself as you are, whilst having compassion for yourself as you strive to become the best you can be, you are heading in the right direction.

I hope that you now have a deeper understanding of why support is such an essential part of your business, but you might be wondering how you can go from where you are in your life now to setting up your own support network. There is a vast array of options available for both self-support and seeking support from others for your body, mind, and soul. I will share in more detail about the importance of seeking support from others, but for now I will say that this might include reading books, attending training courses, hiring a coach, therapist, or mentors, or having a spiritual practice.

My advice is not to rush these changes, but instead to go at a pace that feels manageable. Once you can adopt new habits in one area of support, you will feel more open and willing to move onto another one. If you had told me one year ago that I would have a morning routine of waking up at 5am, exercising, having a spiritual practice, and making time to learn before I started work, I would have told you to stick your routine where the sun doesn't shine! This is not something that came easily and, full disclosure, sometimes I still sleep through and swear at the alarm. But, hand on heart, I feel a million times better for supporting my body, mind, and soul. I have noticed a decrease in procrastination and an increase in productivity, as well as having a clearer and calmer mind.

To live a successful business life, it is imperative that you have a good balance in all three areas. This will not happen overnight, and I can tell you that it won't be easy. This is a lifelong process that might even get worse before it gets better!

The Freepreneur seeks support from others

Let's get something straight. You (and your ego!) cannot build your business on your own. When things are going well in your business, you may have that awesome superhero feeling where you can take on the world. But if your foundations are built on quicksand instead of solid cement, there will be no successful business. One of the imperative foundations for any successful business is to receive support from others. I understand that the most unnatural words to come out of any entrepreneur's mouth are, 'Please can you help me.' But I want to give you a word of warning. If you decide to ignore this invaluable part of building your business, you can expect to have a disastrous, instead of a successful, business life.

How do I know? Because I learned the hard way. I mentioned in the introduction that I would share how I successfully built my first business, so here it is. When I started my electrical company in 2005, I decided right from the start that my way was the right way. If you remember, it was at the time when I had resigned from my position as an employed sales agent when my boss thought it was acceptable for me to work harder for a decrease in salary. Funnily enough, I didn't think this was acceptable, and decided it was time for me to show him and everyone else who couldn't see my worth, exactly what I was made of. With a bank loan of $2000 and a head full of confidence, I set off on my journey to create a successful business life on my terms.

One of the reasons I believed so strongly in my self-employed venture was that I planned to trade with exactly the same customers who had been buying from me in my employed sales agent role. I had been building great relationships with them for years, and they all loved me (in a professional sense, obviously!). I took my role very seriously, and I not only served their sales needs but also helped them to develop and grow their businesses. As a result, they gained trust and respect in me, which resulted in them placing even more orders, and I became their number one partner from all the sales agents walking through their doors.

I'm smiling now as I remember back to when I would walk out of their premises to see my competitors waiting outside in their cars, not daring to enter whilst I was inside. I had an impeccable reputation and had every faith that this, combined with my strong sales record, would continue to flourish as I set out on my own. To reassure myself that there would be a smooth transition from employed to self-employed success, I spoke to every single one of my customers and told them of my plan. I asked them if they would continue to trade with me once I had my own business. They said yes, yes, and yes! So, I took their word for it and boldly handed in my notice.

I was yet to test my wings, but I was ready to fly. Little did I know that my wings had actually been clipped and that there was only one person responsible – you guessed it; it was me. I didn't ask anyone else for their opinion on my plan. I didn't ask anyone else for their support. I thought I was indestructible. And I was wrong!

One day after leaving my job, I jumped in my car, drove to see my first customer, and literally bounced into their office. I couldn't wait to tell them the good news, 'Bodo is back! I have a brand-new company and I'm ready for business. What would you like to buy?' I waited in anticipation for a few moments whilst expecting to take a large order on my first day. What I wasn't expecting was the confusion from my customer, who replied, "Err, well, you tell me. What can you sell?"

I replied with confidence, 'I can sell you anything. Just tell me what you want.'

He replied, "Bodo, with your old company you would have a complete price list, you would visit with flyers filled with special offers – it was very clear on *how* I could buy from you. But now I'm not so sure we can continue working together like this."

Inside my head I was screaming, *what do you mean we can't work together like this? Come on! What do you mean it's not clear? You said you were going to buy from me and now you're not. I thought we had an agreement. Why are you going back on your word!?* At this point, I could feel that I would not be leaving with an order so I (and my bruised ego) walked out, muttering a few swear words under my breath as I did! (Side note: Anyone else smell a victim?)

My pride may have been a little dented, but I told myself that this was only one customer. Maybe he'd got out of bed on the wrong side that morning. There were plenty more fish in the electrical goods' sea.

I drove to see the next customer and gave them exactly the same sales pitch, and to my surprise they gave me exactly the same reason not to buy from me. This happened over and over and over again as I drove to every single potential customer. And there were 20 customers in total, and more than 1000 miles of driving from city to city, in the longest week of my life. They were all adamant that they didn't want to buy, and I was gutted and confused that they didn't want me to sell.

As I drove home late on the last evening, I knew I needed to find a different approach. So, I decided to be more professional and take the electrical wholesalers' catalogue and price list back to every single customer. Surely, they would want to buy now? Nope. They told me that they were able to buy from the same companies at better prices. Duh! I had made a schoolboy error and had forgotten to ask the customers what they were already paying.

By this point, my stress levels were sky high. I was one month into, supposedly, building my empire, and all I'd achieved was spending half of my bank loan and pissing off my mum and my partner at the time, who had quickly lost their trust in me to provide for the family. If I'm honest, I was also starting to lose trust in myself. I had not only lost a lot of time and money by making poor decisions, but I had also lost a lot of self-esteem and confidence.

The easy option would have been to give up, but I was determined that the word 'quit' was not going to enter my vocabulary. I had to take responsibility for the fact that I had resigned from an employed position with little financial security and no start-up action plan. After initially sulking that my potential customers had 'gone back on their word', I also had to take responsibility for the fact that they didn't know that I would be changing the rules and that I wouldn't have a solid sales strategy in place.

I had to admit that in order for my business to succeed, I needed to swap being stubborn for seeking some support. In my quest for answers, I decided to take the unusual approach of searching for an informative business book. (You may be wondering why this was unusual, but back in winter 2005-2006, it was rare to find good business books, let alone ones that were translated into Romanian.) As I write this in 2020, I have a collection of over 400 books, but I will never forget reading, *Guerrilla Selling, Unconventional weapons & tactics for increasing your sales,* by Jay Conrad Levinson, that helped me to get out of my stagnant sales rut in 2006. During this time, I also read some articles in the economic Romanian magazine.

Seeking self-support was a step in the right direction, but I knew that I also needed to put my pride to one side and make a phone call to a man who went on to become my business mentor and business partner for many years. Marius Cojocaru had an electrical distribution business, and he agreed that he would supply me with products and teach me how to get started on my own. In exchange, I would place the majority of my orders with his company in the first year. I was open and honest about my challenges, and took his advice on the most popular products, as well as taking on board his guidance about ongoing growth and business development.

With this fresh motivation and support in place, I designed what I now refer to as a Minimum Viable Prototype, and guess what? I made my first sale as an official entrepreneur! (More information on Minimum Viable Prototype, and how you can create one for your business, in the courses available in The Freepreneur Resources). Believe me when I say that this was much more than just a sale to me. Yes, I was over the moon that I had finally made some money. I was elated that the customer thanked me for the great service and wanted to order again, but it was the feeling of validating my business, trusting myself, and seeing the tension ease within my family, that gave me the most satisfaction. Instead of arguing, we were celebrating, and they could see that my hard work and determination had finally paid off.

Thank goodness I didn't listen to the voices in my head which were yelling, 'Are you really built to be an entrepreneur? Have you got the guts to finish what you've started? Do you think you are kidding yourself by believing you have what it takes to make it on your own?' Thank goodness I didn't listen to my friends and my old boss who told me I would never succeed, and who laughed at me when they heard I was going to resign from a well-paid job and stupidly 'risk it all.'

And thank goodness I didn't listen to my ego which was trying to keep me stuck by keeping me safe. In these moments of doubt, I was so close to succumbing to the pressure of going back to follow the crowd, but everything changed when I sought some self-support as well as asking for support from those who were already on the entrepreneurial path. The moral of the story? As my confidence, faith, and support continued to grow, so did my business.

It's funny how, as children, we continually ask for help and think nothing of it, but at some stage in growing up we develop the misconception that asking for support can be seen as a weakness. More often than not, we need to reach our 'enough is enough' moment before we finally reach out for support.

This is why it is so important to have a close and supportive group of people around you as you evolve. Be honest with them and share that you are embarking on this journey and want to be the best you can be. Who knows, you may even inspire them to make some positive improvements in their life, too!

It's sad but true that the majority of the support you think you will receive will not materialise. This can be very disheartening, especially in the early days of your business. Many entrepreneurs, including myself, have not always had support from close friends and family. This is why it is even more important to seek external support in the form of a coach or a business mentor. Please stay away from the opinions of people who aren't entrepreneurs. The simple reason is because they are not in the arena.

'A lot of cheap seats in the arena are filled with people who never venture onto the floor. They just hurl mean-spirited criticisms and put-downs from a safe distance.

For me, if you're not in the arena getting your ass kicked, I'm not interested in your feedback.'

Brené Brown, Daring Greatly, Penguin Life: 2015

If you have a supportive family and/or spouse who is in the arena, appreciate them and keep them close! If you don't, the answer is not to sulk about your expectations not being met, but instead commit that nothing and nobody will stop you from achieving your goals.

Once you have built or reached a support network, you are well on your way to building a successful business.

The Freepreneur seeks their own support

You now know that I wholeheartedly recommend seeking support from others, but it is also imperative that you also seek support from yourself.

Another time when I reached an 'enough is enough' moment was in 2002, when I began suffering from crippling panic attacks. Having been told that my doctor couldn't help me, I decided that I would do whatever it took to support my own mind. In my eyes, I had two choices. I could either carry on the way I was, being ruled by something that was controlling me, or I could take responsibility for my lifestyle choices and take the control back.

Through trial, error, and sheer desperation, I discovered that falling asleep was the quickest way to relieve my symptoms. As soon as I felt the first signs coming on, I would run back to my house, get in bed, and fall fast asleep. In the moment I fell asleep, it was like I had activated a panic attack reset button. I would sleep for 20 minutes and wake up feeling calm again. Once I had regained this control, I researched and learned some relaxation breathing techniques. I also discovered that drinking too much coffee, having too much stress, and not getting enough sleep in the evening, were also triggers for an attack. By supporting myself and implementing new healthy lifestyle habits, I was able to gradually reduce and then completely eliminate the panic attacks that had the potential to put a huge strain on my emotional wellbeing. Having just shared how I introduced some new healthy lifestyle habits in 2002, it may surprise you that in 2016 I was smoking at least 50, yes 50, cigarettes every single day! And that was just the real ones; in between those nicotine fixes, I was also smoking E-cigarettes. As you can imagine this not-so-healthy habit was not just costing me a lot of money, it was also costing me a lot of lost time in productivity.

This was the factor that caused me to research some self-support to finally quit after 21 long years of being a smoker. I read a book that shared a proven process; I began reading as a slightly sceptical smoker and finished reading as a fully believing non-smoker! This change in my lifestyle, combined with some stomach problems, led me to re-assess my eating habits and in 2017 I became a vegetarian.

Over the last few years, I have continued to strive to support myself in all areas of my life. I now prioritise my physical, emotional, and spiritual wellbeing, and know that taking this responsibility has had a huge positive impact on not only my business but also my personal life. I have happily invested a lot of money in my training and education, as well as paying for coaches and therapists. The result? I am shining brightly right now. I am physically healthier, I have a much more balanced emotional state of mind, and my confidence and self-esteem have increased, which enables me to be on top form in my mission to make a difference in the world.

Incorporating all of this support in my life has helped to make me finally feel complete. Despite writing this book in the middle of a global pandemic, life is pretty damn amazing. I know that I could not have reached this point on my own by believing that my way was the only way. When I look back at the man I once was, I see so much lost time by not looking after myself. It was naive of me to think that I could make a difference in the world without first making a difference to myself.

You may have recognised yourself in parts of my story, which is great self-awareness, but awareness is not enough to make positive changes in your life. It's important that you take a good, honest look at the different areas of your own life and ask yourself how you could take steps to improve and strengthen these. (Take a look to the Resources section on the website for a list of in-depth support.)

Seeking support from others and providing support for yourself is not an option for success, it is a necessity!

Secret #19

The Freepreneur understands their purpose

If you feel you are getting closer to identifying your business idea, this next section will bring you greater clarity.

What is your why?

If you don't yet have an idea, maybe this is the missing piece that you've been waiting for? Before I share the formula, which is now known about and used all over the world, I'd like to share the process I followed which finally allowed me to discover the business that really set my soul on fire.

I want to take you back to late 2012. I had begun to get my life back on track after the devastating impact of losing my first business, and I had started to have some ideas which led to the start-up of some new businesses. From the outside looking in, things looked good: business momentum was building, and I was starting to earn good money again. So, why did I feel empty on the inside? Because my business was not aligned with my body, soul, and spirit. Yes, there was profit, but there was no passion.

I followed my intuition and started to dig deeper into how I could set up a business that filled both my soul and my bank balance. Was that even possible? I started to make a list of all of the activities that I loved to do, e.g. I loved to teach people; I loved to speak in front of audiences; I loved to be the centre of attention; I loved to share my learnt wisdom and guidance with others; I loved to start new businesses; I loved to share with others the results of starting new businesses; I loved to meet new people; I loved to visit new places; I loved to start new ventures; I loved to test new business ideas, to name just a few.

After I filled up the list with tens of activities that I loved, I analysed my findings and tried to figure out what business I could start that would mix all of these activities together. It was clear that an educational and consultancy business helping people start and grow their businesses would be the perfect combination of them all.

The next question was what skills would I need to have to be successful, and even to become number one in this business? So, I made another list. This time I wrote down the knowledge, skills, and competencies needed, then I divided them into what I was good at, and the activities that I needed to learn in order to be successful. My mission was to then bridge the gap by learning how to become the best I could be in each activity that I loved.

I then made a third list of what I felt the world needs – and I was in luck, as the world definitely needs more successful business owners! This process led me to my decision to become an influencer in entrepreneurship and teaching others how to start or improve their business in the first few years of trading. I'll be honest, I didn't write on my list that I would love to write a book to inspire others, but the fact that I am doing so now tells me that my process works!

It wasn't until a few years later that I discovered the similar concept, known as Ikigai, has been taught for many years.

Definition of Ikigai – from Wikipedia

Ikigai is a Japanese concept that means 'a reason for being'. The word refers to having direction or purpose in life, that which makes one's life worthwhile, and towards which an individual takes spontaneous and willing actions, giving them satisfaction and a sense of meaning to life.

It is said that your ikigai is what gets you up every morning and keeps you going. It encourages you to combine what you love, what you're good at, what the world needs, and what you can get paid for. Once you have achieved this, you have found your ikigai! There have been many studies around this, and one theory is that ikigai can make you live longer, with more direction. I encourage all of my clients to search deep for these answers. When you can combine these four elements into your business, you are well on your way to achieving a successful business life on your terms.

Find your ikigai and take the necessary action to achieve it!

Secret #20

The Freepreneur builds 'vehicles' to create and maintain freedom

I remember back when I started my first company in 2005, I wanted to build an empire that gave me both more money and more power. I achieved both, but in doing so I also inadvertently built myself a self-contained prison. Right from the very beginning, I always knew that I wanted to do (and control) everything – and I mean everything. For the first five years, I was the office manager, the sales manager, the marketing manager, the buyer, the accountant, the lawyer, the delivery driver, and of course, the very important role of being the cleaner! Why? I had once heard the saying that to become an effective leader you need to be prepared to do *anything* in your business – and yes, this included cleaning the office toilet!

I wanted to become a great leader, but it appears that I may have misinterpreted this advice because I took the guidance literally. I did it all, day by day (and often through the night) and started to build my business along with the invisible walls of my very own prison.

If I'm honest, I wanted to feel in control. After all, my driving force for leaving life as an employee was so that I could be in control of my life and not answer to someone else. My business was my baby, and I wanted to be the one to nurture it. When I became exhausted from working every hour that God sent, I finally came to the conclusion that I needed to delegate something. But instead of delegating the work in the office (I wanted to still be in control of that), I decided to employee a new sales agent. Despite knowing that this was the right thing to do, my ego did not like it, so it came up with a short checklist: the new sales agent could not be as good as I was; and it had to be someone I knew. So, I hired my cousin.

I trained him and, to be fair, he became a very good sales agent. Life was going to become easier now, surely? Nope. I was stuck in the office, drowning in paperwork, still in the prison, whilst he was out and about having a great time. I gave my ego a talking-to and decided to hire an office manager to free up some more of my time. Great idea, right? Wrong. I still could not let go of the control. Despite giving training on how to place orders, I still needed to supervise and oversee Every. Single. Task.

One of the most stressful areas of my work was managing the company's cash flow. We were fortunate to buy our goods on 90-day payment terms. The plan was to sell them at a profit before our invoices were due, and *cha-ching,* the money would roll in. The challenge was that the plan did not always go to plan, and the unpredictable cash flow left me with a false sense of security. I was never fully aware of the true financial position of the company, but this didn't stop me from spending lots of money from the increasing turnover.

I will admit that I loved the power that money brought, and I enjoyed the social competition of always having the best of everything. I wanted to have the best car, the best apartment, the best penthouse, the best holidays, not to mention the best bling when it came to designer watches and jewellery. I was not only living within the walls of an invisible prison, I was also living within a very pretentious bubble that, unbeknown to me, was about to spectacularly burst.

I could feel the pressure mounting but there was a part of me that just couldn't let go. My workload, stress levels, and prison walls, were all increasing day by day. If I'm honest, I was in a worse position than when I'd been an employee, because now I was carrying out the roles of five other people!

I began to feel trapped. At one point, I decided enough was enough, and in 2010 I decided that my escape was going to come in the form of starting a new life in Australia. The immigration forms were completed and sent off, and I eagerly awaited their reply. But I was declined the right to enter, as I failed their English test by half a point! Half a bloody point, can you believe it?! I was angry. I kept on asking myself why this had happened (of course, I now know that the Universe had a bigger plan, and for this I am grateful). I kept a strong smile on my face for the outside world to see, but on the inside, I was starting to break. I didn't have enough time for myself, my family, my friends, or to develop and grow myself personally or professionally.

I would love to tell you that I found the courage and self-awareness to make some much-needed changes, but having read this far you already know how the story ends. It was a combination of juggling the unpredicted cashflow and some unfortunate and unforeseen events that led to someone else tearing down my prison walls with no warning. I had no choice but to break free. Everything spiralled out of control and led to the collapse of my business and, ultimately, my life, which was when I found myself feeling alone and ashamed lying on the sofa in 2011.

At the peak of my business success, I accomplished my goal of earning more money. I also thought I had found happiness by increasing my power as well as my control, but it wasn't true happiness. Somewhere along the way, I lost my direction and I forgot about my feelings, my emotions, my health, my soul, my desires, and more importantly, my freedom.

If you are reading this now – as an employee, freelancer, or as an entrepreneur – and recognise yourself within this story, my guidance to you is this: Take action now to create your freedom. Do not wait until the prison walls are so high that your world becomes a very dark place to live. Turn on the lights, fast.

The first step to take is to admit the walls are there in the first place and not to be annoyed at yourself if this is the case. You have worked incredibly hard and have always done your best. I want you to ask yourself, honestly, do you want to change?

This may seem like a silly question, which I will elaborate on in a moment, but for now I want you think about how your professional and your personal life will look in one year's time if nothing changes. How about three or even five years' time? Will your life be the same, or will it be even worse? You may be wondering how it could be worse. Take a look at the people who are around you, the people who you love and care about. Ask yourself, do you still want these people to be in your life whilst having a close and fulfilled relationship? The chances are that they will see the prison walls before you do. They may become tired of giving unrequited love to a prisoner and feeling like they are an option, not a priority, in your life. Because all the love in the world cannot continuously penetrate through the dark prison walls. The good news is that it's not too late. Break down the walls, let in the light, and let in the love.

If, on the other hand, you are genuinely happy with always being 'busy', you don't have a problem with shutting yourself off, and having a loving and fulfilling relationship is not high up on your list of priorities, then that's ok. There is no judgement; it is your choice and it is your life.

But if you are craving more freedom, you need to stop fighting and let go of the control! Outsource your work to freelancers, install effective systems, processes, bots, and funnels, to take the pressure off you. Ask yourself why you started in the first place: was it for more time, to have better quality relationships, or perhaps to be a role model and to make a difference? When you deeply connect with your values, you can base all of your future decisions around this. When I am now looking at new business opportunities, I always ask myself if this venture will create freedom, or will it create prison walls for me?

Having learnt the hard way and rebuilt my life, I now understand that the most important part of business success is having freedom. Freedom in your thinking, your feelings, your emotions, as well as freedom in how, with whom, and where you choose to live your life. This is now the purpose and the centre of everything I teach my students and clients. I empower them to transform and leverage their ideas into building not only a business, but a vehicle to create their own freedom. And that is priceless. Hitting rock bottom in my life means that I can now teach entrepreneurs how to set the solid foundations for success. And this brings me so much joy and fulfilment. Even when my first business appeared to be successful, I always felt like there was a missing piece. Fulfilment was the missing piece that no amount of money could buy. When you follow your heart and run a business on your terms, fulfilment is also yours for the taking.

I am still on my journey, but I have never felt so passionate about sharing the secrets of how to build a successful business life on your own terms.

You may be wondering how the story ends? Have I found the peace, contentment, and freedom I was searching for? Have I built my own vehicle(s) for success?

Are you sitting comfortably? Then all will be revealed…

August 2020

Enough is enough! I knew what I needed to do. I was about to make a decision that would change my life as I knew it, and I was ready. Have you ever had a deep knowing that something needs to change in your life? At first, it lingers with such a quiet gentleness that you barely notice it's there, but as time passes the feeling refuses to go away. It gets bigger and louder, taking up so much space that you are finally forced to take notice. Try as you might, you just can't ignore it any longer.

Growing up, I had always felt an attraction towards the life of the travelling gypsies. They had their home and all of their belongings safely packed away in their horse and carriage as they travelled from place to place whenever they chose. They lived life on their terms, and nothing came between them and their freedom. I have often wondered if I was perhaps a nomad gypsy in my past life, as no matter where I have lived, this fascination has always stayed with me. But along with the majority of the population, I conformed to the standards that society expected and was worked hard to create security, not freedom.

Looking back, I can see that by becoming a salesman, a business development manager and an entrepreneur who travelled from town to town, perhaps I was trying to emulate the freedom of the gypsy nomad lifestyle – but it was never enough. The longing never subsided and the knowing never disappeared.

In March 2020, when our country went into full lockdown due to the Corona virus, I was unable to leave my apartment in Bucharest for 24 hours a day, 66 days in a row. If I did leave, it was mandatory to have a very good reason and write an official declaration stating where I was going and why. I tried to remain positive, but not being able to have my freedom, combined with not being able to see the people I cared about, was hard.

Perhaps being forced to stay at home was the final trigger to really set myself free. This challenging time gave me the opportunity to reflect on what was important and encouraged me to reassess how I wanted to live my life once the lockdown was eased. I had already adapted and changed how I ran my business, but now it was time to adapt and change how I lived my life. It was time to follow my heart and fulfil the need and the knowing that had been buried deep within me for far too long.

I had been thinking for a while about different ways to embrace more freedom into my life, but everything was accelerated in July when my landlord called me to discuss my rental contract, which was due to renew in one month's time. He had been very accommodating during the crisis but advised that should I wish to continue being a tenant, there would be an increase in my rent.

That was the moment I knew. I felt it like a bullet. To be fair, the increase wasn't a huge amount, but my ego (or maybe my soul?) kicked in and said no! Enough is enough. It's time to go. I don't want to live here anymore. But where will I go?

Maybe I could move to the seaside, or to the mountains, or to another city in Romania? Maybe I could move to London? Or Edinburgh, or maybe Sydney? And that's when the possibility dawned on me... what if I could stay in all of these places?

I did some calculations and worked out how much I was paying for my current bills, and realised that for the same amount, or potentially even less, I could rent many different apartments and still have everything I needed. Ok, so maybe it wouldn't be possible to travel worldwide until the international restrictions were lifted, but there were still so many places to visit in Romania.

My mind was made up. I was going to embark on a new journey to satisfy my soul like never before. After many years of searching in the wrong places, I was going to find my own freedom. I was going to become a nomad.

I picked up the phone and called my landlord. I thanked him for his support and told him of my decision to end the tenancy. Wow, this was really happening! I didn't for one-minute doubt my decision, but in that moment a few questions flashed into my mind.

How will I continue to earn money?

Thankfully, I had moved all of my businesses online during lockdown, which meant that as long as I had a smartphone, a laptop, and an internet connection, I could work from any location in the world. Since I started to write this book, I had also decided to build The Freepreneur movement. My vision is to bring together a supportive worldwide community where I will share valuable content through my blogs and vlogs, whilst working with a remote team of freelancers. Well, this is the perfect opportunity to get started!

What will other people say about my decision?

Well, I guess the clue is in the last two words of the heading: 'my decision'. I am trying to live my life on my terms, not based on what other people think. I don't say this in a rude, arrogant, or hurtful way. I say this with confidence that I am done with living a life based on other people's expectations.

I want to be a role model for other people to be true to themselves, but how can I accomplish this if I'm not true to myself? Yes, people will talk. So what? Let them talk. Yes, it may be seen as a controversial decision, but I am used to that. I have 'friends' from childhood who over the last few years have told me that I am crazy and that I need to see a psychiatrist! I even had some family members who didn't understand my journey, but they saw me rebuilding my life and slowly became curious and supportive of what I was doing.

What I have learnt is that when you follow your own path, some people will come with you and others will fall away, but either way that's ok. I will not allow other people's negative thoughts to get in the way of my purpose.

What about my kids?

This is one of the main reasons why I *need* to do this, to show them that they, too, can live life on their terms. Think of the amazing adventures we could have together if they were to come and stay. And it goes without saying that I will continue to visit and play a supportive role in their lives, no matter where I am in the world.

Now that I had full confidence that any challenges that look like disadvantages could be turned into advantages, the next step was to buy a new car – a convertible, to be precise. (Well, much as a horse and carriage would be fun for a while, I needed something a bit more practical!)

By chance, one of my neighbours had a Ford Focus convertible for sale, and would you believe, it was exactly the same model as the car I'd owned ten years ago! In the midst of the chaos in 2011, when my life was collapsing around my feet, I drove home one evening and parked my car outside my house. I woke up in the morning, looked out of my window and the car was gone! I initially thought it had been stolen, but later found out that it had probably been taken back into the possession of the leasing company. If I hadn't felt like a big enough let down to my family already, this humiliation certainly rubbed a lot of salt into my wound – a wound that nine years later was still unhealed.

When I saw the same car for sale, I was optimistic that it would tick all of my boxes: a) It was a car; b) It was a convertible; c) It had a large boot; d) It would heal my wound and give me closure on that memory.

You may think that 'd' sounds a little strange, but I'm sure I'm not the only one who has contemplated making a purchase to heal a wound. There are many people who are aware of their past wounds, but not so many people who are prepared to revisit and heal them. I once read an anonymous quote that said, 'If you don't heal your wounds, you will bleed onto someone who didn't cut you.' It's powerful, and it's true.

I arranged to meet the seller of the Ford Focus CC, and everything looked great. He allowed me to spend some time in the car on my own, whilst I checked everything out, reminisced, and listened to some music. I made him aware of a few concerns and he agreed to have the repairs carried out before the sale went ahead.

Long story short, he didn't keep his promise and the sale didn't go ahead. Was I disappointed? Not at all. Especially when I realised that spending that time in the car on my own had been enough to heal my wound from the past. I have complete faith in the direction in which I am guided and firmly believe in the saying, 'What's for you won't pass you by'. I trusted that there was a better car waiting, and I was right.

A few days later, one of my clients, Dan Vache, who has a company that specialises in helping customers to buy good second-hand cars, suggested that I looked at a Mini Cooper Cabriolet. I loved that it was a stylish and classic car, but having known someone who used to own one, I wasn't so enthusiastic about the size of the boot. I decided to put my doubts to one side and view the car with an open mind. I wasn't disappointed with the outside, it was beautiful. But what about the boot?

I tried to remain positive as I opened it, but it wasn't just small… it was damn small! I silently asked myself how I would fit all my things in. As if to read my thoughts, the owner said, 'Come on, let's go for a drive, you will love it. It's like driving a go-kart.' My enthusiasm returned. Having driven many go-karts throughout my childhood, this sparked a glimmer of hope and a curiosity within me. Having driven a million kilometres over the last 15 years, I had to admit that I had fallen out of love with driving. Could this test drive recapture my love?

What can I say? It was love at first pedal! He was right. The sensation of the acceleration, combined with the movement of the gears and the interior sports set-up, reminded me of the feeling I had as a child when I was racing go-karts. Ten minutes later, we had agreed the sale, and any concerns I'd had about the small boot had disappeared as I had a revelation. If ***my things*** don't fit into the boot, then ***they're not my things***. It was a very liberating moment. Surely all I would need are a few clothes, a few toiletries, the books I am currently reading, my essential documents, and two towels. Simple.

I mean, why do we accumulate so much crap in the first place? Let's take cups and glasses as an example – we have different glasses for shots, whisky, white wine, red wine, juice, water, beer, cocktails, tea, espresso, brandy, and lattes! Why? Because we never know who maybe, one day, possibly, will decide that they might want to come to our house, and perhaps they could be thirsty and might want a drink. We don't know which drink they want, or their preference to what they will drink it from, so we cover all eventualities and buy six of everything! Why? Because we accumulate and keep what we *think* we need.

I'm going to let you into a (bonus!) secret… I have discovered that you don't need all of the glasses. That's right, ladies and gentlemen, you heard it here first. You can, in fact, drink wine out of a juice glass! I have tried it and, granted, it was a little strange at first, but only because we have been programmed not to change. So, here's the thing: if you can change your drinking habits, you can also change your buying habits! And when you take this approach, it gives you a whole new perspective on everything in your house. You can literally cut out the crap and concentrate on 'the things' that are really important – not only in your house, but also in your life.

This newfound space allows you to make room for the important people, habits, thoughts, feeling, emotions, and activities, that *really* matter in your life. And that is the moment when you truly begin to step into the world of freedom and happiness. I have so much more to share about this theory (perhaps I should write another book!?), but for now let's get back to preparing for my journey…

Embracing minimalism is a simple theory, but in reality, the practical process of getting rid of years' worth of possessions didn't feel quite so simple at first. I had an entire library of over 400 books, an entire wardrobe packed full of expensive clothes, not to mention an entire apartment full of household goods.

When I started with my books, the questions began. What if I wanted to read them again? Maybe I should replace them by investing in a Kindle, but was it important to invest in 400 Kindle books? No! What I needed to do was change the habit of buying them. I decided that I would buy them only when I wanted to read them, one at a time. But what if I forgot what books I had, should I make a list or a picture? No! I had to trust that the books I had read had given me what I needed and that it was time to donate them to someone else who would enjoy them as much as I had.

This process made me realise that whenever I was feeling stuck, I just needed to ask myself some good questions to help me make a decision and move forward. This has truly helped me to understand the quote from Tony Robbins: 'The quality of your life is a direct reflection of the quality of the questions you are asking yourself.'

You could say that to make things easier I could have stored some items, but I knew this wasn't the answer. It was all or nothing; it would either fit in the small (but perfectly formed) boot, or it wasn't mine to keep.

Once I reminded myself of this decision, I found the clearing process so much easier and I began to donate many more items. But I will be honest, there were some items which weren't quite so easy to detach of. Having read my story, you will have gained an understanding of what a huge part music has played in my life. From a young boy who listened for hours in his bedroom, to a grown man who listened for hours in his apartment. Through the highs and the lows, the tears and the laughter, music has always been a constant in my life.

I had spent a lot of money on buying a good stereo, as the sensation of listening to the crystal-clear sounds felt so good. For a moment, I contemplated whether I could really donate it. Maybe I should just lend it to someone, and that way I could have it back if I needed it. No! Why not donate that beautiful feeling to someone else and make another person happy?! So, that's what I did.

The other challenging decision was whether to keep my beloved suits. I am sure that I am not alone in admitting that I am very attached to my clothes, and in particular my tailor-made suits. If you have ever seen me speak on television or at an event until August 2020, I can almost guarantee that I will have been dressed in a full suit. In fact, it was only two weeks ago that I wore one, but if I'm honest, something felt different then. They're not my style anymore. They are part of the old Bodo; they are part of who I was. So, why was it so hard to part with them? I worked extremely hard to get them, they were each made to fit, and are each worth thousands of euro. I also love the feeling of wearing them and they had become part of my brand, but something was changing…

A few weeks ago, I visited one of the most expensive law firms in Bucharest with one of my clients. On the morning of the meeting, I was getting dressed when I said to myself, *Should I go in a suit or in smart, but casual clothes?* It was a warm day, so I decided on wearing a polo shirt and smart shorts. On our arrival, we were met by two lawyers who, before welcoming us, had already looked us up and down from head to toe.

I smiled politely as I looked around their very posh office. In that moment, I saw all of my past attachments, as well as the person who I had been – the person who defines himself on *things*. The meeting progressed, and at one stage I asked some questions about a particular service. The answer was for that particular service I would need to leave my car keys behind! The lawyer came very close to asking what car I was driving and was serious that we would need to leave our car keys as a deposit! At that point, the cheeky me couldn't help but ask, 'So, maybe I should have worn my bespoke suit today?' (You know my style!)

They were a little lost for words and went on to share how important clothes were blah, blah, blah… but by that point I was smiling, silently thanking them for an experience that had helped me to be very clear in my mind about what was important. I remember thinking, *so this is how people are acting when they are living in a self-imposed prison. A prison of clothes and a prison of a corporation.* I don't want to be a part of that world and was pleased that I had found the courage not to conform. Bodo – 1; Posh solicitors – 0. *Touché*!

Before I made my final decision, I asked my friends, should I burn my suits? They were shocked. Their answer, 'What? No! Don't do it! You better donate them!' And so, I did.

My last concern was, would people judge me, as a business owner, according to my clothes? This was a negative thought that I quickly deleted. There are many people who will not judge me or anyone else based on their clothes. There are examples of very famous people who wear the clothes they choose, not the clothes they are expected to wear. From now on, I will be following their example. No more suits, no more ties. Part of me felt relieved, as this meant there would be more space in the boot of the Bodomobile! I reminded myself that I am an exceptional business coach, so if anyone wants to judge me, they can judge me on my exceptional results!

I am now only 24 hours away from leaving my apartment, when I will be packing my (very small!) bags into my (very small!) boot. A whole new chapter awaits…

Am I fearful? Nope, I am genuinely excited. I love meeting new people and knowing that I can live life like a millionaire, without being a millionaire, is something that fills me with gratitude.

As I prepare to hand back the keys to my apartment, I can't help but reflect on how much my life has changed. It was almost ten years ago that I left my old apartment with my head hung low. I was bitter, angry, and ashamed, as I walked away from my old life feeling like a failure. Tomorrow, I will be driving away from my apartment with my head held high. I feel empowered, proud, and free, as I step into my new life feeling like a winner.

Will I cope without *my things*? Of course! You do not need to own *things* to feel successful; you only need to own your emotions and your feelings. My advice is to fill your life with meaningful moments, not meaningless things. In fact, you do not need to feel attached to things, places, customers, products, or people…

The Freepreneur only feels attached to freedom!

Once you have grasped this concept, as well as implementing the secrets I have shared, *that* is when you will truly feel liberated.

What's next?

Now that you have embraced the Freepreneur Mindset, it is time for you to master the Freepreneur Business Method and implement the Freepreneur Business Tools that will help you build your business life on your terms. These will be covered in the next two parts of this trilogy, and also in my courses.

Please visit https://thefreepreneur.eu/book-resources to find details about my courses and for exclusive bonuses and discounts for you, as a reader of this book. I encourage you to start with downloading and printing The Freepreneur Mindset Manifesto™ and The Freepreneur Ultimate Manifesto™.

The Freepreneur Mindset Manifesto

I am a Freepeneur
I have an investor attitude
I love and accept myself unconditionally
I let go of grudges
I am defined by my present
I release any negativity from my life
I celebrate the success of others
I trust myself as well as others
I overcome Impostor Syndrome
I embrace failure as well as success
I refuse to play the victim role
I am empathetic
I have an abundance mindset
I embrace feedback
I am in love with solving customers' problems
I fulfil my dreams
I am laser-focused
I understand how to manage risk
I support my body, mind, and soul
I understand my purpose
I build 'vehicles' to create and maintain my freedom

The Freepreneur Ultimate Manifesto

I am a Freepeneur

I refuse to sell my time for money, control and constant praise

I choose carefully why, where, when, with whom and how to invest my resources

I aim for the lowest risk and investment against the highest return possible

I choose evergreen instead of ephemeral

I feed my wallet and starve my ego

I choose freedom instead of control

Acknowledgments

To George, Miriam and Sonia, thank you for inspiring me to be the best (dad) I can be. To my mum, the best mum in the world, thank you for everything! I hope you are proud (again) now.

Along with my closest family members there are hundreds, if not thousands, of wonderful people I have met throughout my life who helped me a lot with their wisdom, patience, love, energy and awesome life lessons. I don't want to miss anyone, so I have chosen not to try and name you all. But be sure that without all of you, I would not be the person I am today, and this book would not have been possible. I feel so lucky to have met so many wonderful people and I thank you all, no matter the type of relationship we have had. If you are reading this and have met me before or during the process of writing this book, these words are for you. God bless you!

Sometimes in our life someone appears who will change it forever. In the same way that a spark transforms the sawdust into fire, Cassandra, my beloved ghostwriter and friend, changed my life forever. She helped me to get this book out of my soul so that I could share it with you and to the world. Because this is her blessing. To help people heal their soul through writing an awesome book that will help other people and create a ripple of empowerment. You are the kindest, supportive and understanding person I have ever met in my life. Thank you from the bottom of my soul and may The Healing Force be with you.

I would like to say a big thank you to Christine McPherson for editing my book.

I would like to convey my special thanks to Roxana Zelinca from Corealy for designing the amazing cover of this book. She answered with a big YES to my call for a cover designer and helped me a lot. You can contact her at roxana.zelinca@gmail.com

Graphics designed by Freepik was integrated in the book cover.

A special thank you...

There are some special people that I would like to mention because they said a big YES in supporting me and this book, so I have the following list of sponsors and cheerleaders.

To Lucian, my first and biggest sponsor in this journey. Thank you for all your support in my entrepreneurial education and for inspiring me to what a truly Freepreneur should be. The way you build your business in the last almost 30 years, growing and prospering in a market dominated by corporations is an example for every aspiring Freepreneur. Even though I wouldn't be able to list all of the good things I learnt from you, I do know that there were many, so I thank you from the bottom of my heart. May your best years start today and may the Freedom Force be forever with you!

A big and special thank you for Madalina Tanase, a very active Romanian Environmental Activist. As a sponsor of this book, she would like to share this message with all of you:

"Humbleness, Generousness, Nomadness, Freepreneurness makes the world circular. Bodo Codreanu leads from his soul, and through his online courses he has taught me to do the same as a future Freepreneur. His vast business experience with successes and failures, made me realize that the Environmental Activist battle in myself and the fight with my savior personality type, can be a wonderful mix that can be brought to reality through green sustainable business implemented step by step into my own projects as part of Circular Business Economy. Bodo and his startup team from www.wastebill.ro inspired me when they implemented, through their affinity for this domain, a great platform for the Romanian B2B market created for the environmental consultants and those responsible for recording, managing and reporting company environmental obligations.

I would have loved to tell you exactly who I am or why am I here, but by the time when you read this maybe I will change 3 business domain activities as I have done in the last 10 years – from a national tour guide to working in the IT field speaking in Dutch, to Service Desk IT support, to a IoT Preventive Maintenance Engineer and now into sustainability projects. The most important thing is that I am always reinventing myself and learning from the Universal vibes that we create and from the people we attract in our lives."

You can contact Madalina by email: madalinattanase@gmail.com

Madalina, thank you for your support, you are an amazing and warm soul! May the Environmental Force be with you!

A big thumbs up for Elena Bita, HR director in a multinational company & independent HR consultant. As a sponsor, she has asked me to share her beautiful message with you:

"Self-development is coming in ways that you can't imagine sometimes but what is important is to set up your own values and rules that can keep you standing up no matter what. The HR world is full of challenges that provoke both your mindset and your soul. HR is about people first of all and a balance between what is right from others point of view and your reality. Coaching is helping to keep that balance and don't lose yourself in a world of others. Courage is to ask for coaching and have the patience to learn from other people experiences. I think entrepreneurship is the combination between courage, self-development and coaching. This form of freedom offers you the possibility to do what you love and earn money in same time! I wish you courage, patience and kindness for yourself!"

You can contact Elena by email: bitaelena@gmail.com

Elena, thank you for all of your support, you are amazing! May the Coaching Force be with you!

A big thank you to Ionut Costache, owner at VEKROM SERVICES SRL (https://vekrom.ro). As a sponsor, he asked me to share his wonderful message with you:

"I have met Bodo in the most important time of my life, because he was the spark that triggered the desire to take my life in my own hands and to begin this new chapter in entrepreneurship. Freepreneur... I love this concept and I am grateful to Bodo because he managed to take me out from *the safety zone* leaving behind the mentality of an employee and after an experience of over 20 years in the technical field to start the entrepreneurial journey and to give my best in this new chapter - Project Management services at the level of Excellence, by creating a united team around the company's values and through sustainable partnerships. And this is just the first step... due to the technical background in the oil and gas industry, my plan is to develop consultancy services in this field, industrial production and to get involved in social projects, so necessary for the society in which we live."

You can contact Ionut at office@vekrom.ro

Thank you Ionut, you are a warrior, may The Project Management Force be with you!

Special thanks to Gabriel Goncear, an entrepreneur in the field of sales of professional equipment for industry and construction. His company has a team with a wealth of experience in providing integrated technical solutions for fields such as: industry, construction, processing, to name just a few. The specificity of the activity is the offer of professional tools and equipment from well-known manufacturers, which can be purchased or rented, simultaneously providing service, consulting services, commissioning and personal training.

Having the needs of the clients at the center of its activity, the company focuses on ensuring the quality of services provided and developing a long-term partnership. You can find it on https://echipamente-bucuresti.ro

Thank you, Gabriel, may The Startup Force be with you!

Last but not least, many thanks to Mihai Costea, a sponsor for the book and one of my amazing business partners, you are an inspiration for me in so many ways. You were the top student on my business courses, and you inspired me with your unstoppable desire to absorb as much as you could from them in a way that forced me to become a better trainer. Mihai is passionate about coding, personal growth, financial markets and entrepreneurship in such a way that he is investing in, or running successful companies and startups from which I mention https://cosmicweb.ro https://wastebill.ro and https://ergoshop.ro

You can find him by email at office@cosmicweb.ro

Thank you, Mihai, and may The Investing Force be with you!

I will continue by thanking my supporters on this beautiful journey:

Nicoleta Jutka, visual artist, art teacher, designer and owner @ Nicole Jutka Gallery.

Cristina Scomoroscenco, biochemist, cosmetic formulator and founder @ Skincores.

Liliana Talasman entrepreneur and coach at @ Pro Mind Set.

And Nicoleta Nemesi, an aspiring Freepreneur.

I would like to end this section by thanking you, my prelaunch cheerleaders, for your support on this beautiful journey: Camelia Suryani, Andra Lungu, Theodora Macedon, Andreea Georgiana Breazu, Roxana Ichim, Daniela Safta, Cristina Zamfir, Dan Consulea, Dan Vache, Alexandru Rusu, Mihai Dumbrava and Igor Verdes.

I love you all!

About the author

Bodo, now a nomad, is a Freepreneur, author, investor and business coach.

When he's not running business seminars or mentoring entrepreneurs, he can often be found implementing new business ideas, developing start-ups, writing, driving (his Bodomobile!), sailing, swimming, surfing, skiing, biking or hiking throughout the world.

Bodo's mission is to motivate committed individuals who want to leverage their ideas and businesses to become Freepreneurs and live a successful business life on their terms.

If you want to apply to work directly with Bodo or to invite him to a speech or a to an interesting adventure, please send a request to bodo@thefreepreneur.eu

If you want to explore more of his work, or his philosophy on life, or just to digest more of his content please visit: https://bodocodreanu.eu and https://thefreepreneur.eu

The Freepreneur Resources

Exclusive goodies on the bonus page for this book: https://thefreepreneur.eu/book-resources/

More about The Freepreneur Business Method you can find here: https://thefreepreneur.eu/courses/

More about The Freepreneur Business Tools you can find here: https://thefreepreneur.eu/business-tools/

More information about my ghostwriter Cassandra Farren here: www.cassandrafarren.com

You can find the Romanian book *Antreprenoriat* by Marius Ghenea, here: https://bit.ly/3fXludC

More about Doug Richard here: https://en.wikipedia.org/wiki/Doug_Richard

More details about the Executive MBA program at Cotrugli Business School: https://cotrugli.org/emba/

The Cantillon Institute Paris: https://www.thecantillon.com/

You can find Marian Rujoiu on his blog: https://www.marian-rujoiu.ro/

More about Antonio Eram's business: https://netopia-payments.com/

Joe Dispenza's book, *Breaking The Habit of Being Yourself: How to Lose Your Mind and Create a New One*: https://amzn.to/36I2tcc

Stephen Covey's book, *The 7 Habits of Highly Effective People*: https://amzn.to/39yxJfz

You can find more about Georgiana Voinea work here: https://georgianavoinea.ro/

More information about Marius Cojocaru business here: https://cojom.ro/

Jay Conrad Levinson book, *Guerrilla Selling, Unconventional weapons & tactics for increasing your sales*: https://amzn.to/36o0bid

Brene Brown books: https://amzn.to/2JvxwhT

Allan Carr books: https://amzn.to/3fQLtTP

My favourite Ikigai book: https://amzn.to/3fTOt1J

Dan Vache youtube channel: https://bit.ly/2KNjFUR

Tony Robbins official website: https://www.tonyrobbins.com/

Contents

Preface	*- 7 -*
Enough is enough!	*- 9 -*
Where do you begin?	*- 27 -*
Secret #1	*- 31 -*
Secret #2	*- 33 -*
Secret #3	*- 35 -*
Secret #4	*- 37 -*
Secret #5	*- 39 -*
Secret #6	*- 41 -*
Secret #7	*- 45 -*
Secret #8	*- 49 -*
Secret #9	*- 53 -*
Secret #10	*- 57 -*
Secret #11	*- 65 -*
Secret #12	*- 71 -*
Secret #13	*- 77 -*
Secret #14	*- 81 -*
Secret #15	*- 87 -*
Secret #16	*- 95 -*

Secret #17	*- 99 -*
Secret #18	*- 105 -*
Secret #19	*- 121 -*
Secret #20	*- 125 -*
August 2020	*- 131 -*
What's next?	*- 144 -*
The Freepreneur Mindset Manifesto	*- 145 -*
The Freepreneur Ultimate Manifesto	*- 146 -*
Acknowledgments	*- 147 -*
A special thank you…	*- 149 -*
About the author	*- 155 -*
The Freepreneur Resources	*- 156 -*

Printed in Great Britain
by Amazon